WHO IS THE GREATEST OF ALL TIME?

With special thanks to Jamie "The Legend" Evans
of the Langley Academy, who helped us come
up with the idea during an author visit.
MO & SB

First US edition 2026
First published by Walker Books (UK) 2024

Library of Congress Control Number: pending
ISBN 978-1-5362-5294-1 (hardcover)
ISBN 978-1-5362-4891-3 (paperback)

26 27 28 29 30 31 SHD 10 9 8 7 6 5 4 3 2

Printed in Chelsea, MI, USA

This book was typeset in ITC Giovanni.
The illustrations were created digitally.

Candlewick Press
99 Dover Street
Somerville, Massachusetts 02144

www.candlewick.com

EU Authorized Representative: HackettFlynn Ltd,
36 Cloch Choirneal, Balrothery,
Co. Dublin, K32 C942, Ireland.
EU@walkerpublishinggroup.com

THE SOCCER GOAT

MESSI V. RONALDO

MATT OLDFIELD

SETH BURKETT

CANDLEWICK PRESS

CONTENTS

KICKOFF

CHARACTER

SKILLS

HALFTIME

STATS

CONTRIBUTION

EXTRA TIME

SOCCER GOAT MESS

IE SOCCER GOAT MESS

LDO THE SOCCER GOA

RONALDO THE SOCCE

MESSI V. RONALDO TH

OAT MESSI V. RONALD

SOCCER GOAT MESSI

IE SOCCER GOAT MES

LDO THE SOCCER GOA

RONALDO THE SOCCE

MESSI V. RONALDO TH

OAT MESSI V. RONALD

SOCCER GOAT MESSI

IE SOCCER GOAT MES

RONALDO THE SOCCE

MESSI V. RONALDO TH

OAT MESSI V. RONALD

SOCCER GOAT MESSI

IE SOCCER GOAT MESS

LDO THE SOCCER GOA

KICKOFF
THE SOCCER GOAT
RONALDO

WHAT *IS* A SOCCER GOAT?

Hi there, we're Matt and Seth—we're two friends who love soccer. *A lot*. Now, seeing as you're reading this book (thanks, by the way), we're guessing you love soccer too. *Snap!* Welcome to our world . . .

We love playing soccer, watching soccer, and reading about soccer. But most of all, we love *arguing* with each other about soccer.

Matt
Your team is trash! My team would beat your team any day—50–0!

Seth
Matt, that would be the biggest win in soccer history!

Matt
So?!

And our favorite topic to fight over? The soccer GOAT!

Oh yeah, before we go any further, we should issue a very important warning: This book is *not* about animals. Sorry! Don't get us wrong, we do like the goats you find on farms, with their cute, fluffy beards; it's just that we prefer the GOATs you find on the soccer field—the . . .

GREATEST OF ALL TIME.

Yes, we're talking about the smartest, the fastest, the most skillful, and the most successful players to ever grace the beautiful game. There have been some real legends over the years, but we believe that two stand out above the rest . . .

IT'S MESSI V. RONALDO!

LIONEL

MESSI

DATE OF BIRTH	June 24, 1987
BIRTHPLACE	Rosario, Argentina
CURRENT POSITION	Center-forward
CLUBS	· Barcelona (2003–21) · Paris Saint-Germain (2021–23) · Inter Miami (2023–present)
NICKNAMES	Leo · Messidona *La Pulga* (The Flea) The Little Magician · GOAT

CRISTIANO

RONALDO

DATE OF BIRTH	February 5, 1985
BIRTHPLACE	Madeira, Portugal
CURRENT POSITION	Striker
CLUBS	• Sporting Lisbon (2002–03) • Manchester United (2003–09, 2021–22) • Real Madrid (2009–18) • Juventus (2018–21) • Al Nassr (2022–present)
NICKNAMES	Ronnie • CR7 • *El Bicho* (The Bug) • Mr. Champions League • GOAT

So, go on then . . . Who is the number one, the best of the best, the ultimate soccer GOAT?

Seth
That's obvious. It's Ronaldo, duh! Let's just agree on that and save ourselves a whole lot of writing.

Matt
Whoa, hold on a moment—
I disagree! Messi is the GOAT.

Seth
What, that little Argentinian who can only use his left foot? Who's always had amazing teammates and never had to work for his success?

Matt
You mean that little Argentinian who's won everything, including the World Cup?

Seth
Whatever! We're going to have to write the rest of this book, aren't we?

Matt
We are. I'll write in favor of Messi.

Seth
And I'll write in favor of Ronaldo. And we'll let the reader decide.

Matt
Finally, something we agree on.

Don't worry, it isn't just us who can't agree on the question of the ultimate soccer GOAT. Soccer fans and players alike all join in on this debate. Which is why this book is all about helping *you* to answer it. We're going to compare Messi and Ronaldo—judging them head-to-head on a range of different qualities. Let's take a closer look at the categories.

WHAT MAKES A SOCCER GOAT?

THEIR CHARACTER

We'll look at the mental side of the game—personality, mindset, and leadership.

THEIR SKILLS

We'll study the full soccer skill set—physical, technical, and tactical skills. And then we'll give you a halftime break.

THEIR STATS

Next up, we'll analyze the numbers—the goals and assists, the individual awards, and the team trophies.

THEIR CONTRIBUTION

We'll end by looking at the bigger picture—how our GOATs have transformed their clubs, their countries, and the beautiful game itself!

And who knows what might happen in extra time? Exciting, right? But before we officially let the battle begin, it's time to learn all about the early lives and careers of our GOATs.

ORIGIN STORIES: LIONEL MESSI

It all began in Rosario, Argentina, with the best birthday present ever: a soccer ball! So what if Leo was only three years old and the ball reached up past his knees? It went everywhere with him, glued to his little left foot.

By the age of five, Leo was already dribbling his way past friends and family on the local dirt playing fields, and scoring goal after goal for Grandoli, his very first soccer team. With his parents working hard to look after him and his brothers, it was his grandmother Celia who usually took him to training and cheered him on from the sidelines.

Did you know? Leo's favorite goal celebration—pointing to the sky with both hands—is a tribute to his grandmother, who sadly died when he was only ten years old.

By his seventh birthday, Leo was ready for his next challenge: playing for Newell's Old Boys, the biggest club in Rosario and his father's favorite team. At Newell's, Leo's rapid rise continued. Over the next six years, he scored nearly five hundred goals, leading his team to every available trophy. People were soon calling him "The Little Magician" and even "Little Maradona"—after Diego Maradona, Argentina's greatest-ever soccer player (more about him later!). That was a big nickname to live up to, but Messi seemed to have it all: speed, skill, unbelievable ball control, a beautiful left foot, and a relentless will to win.

Well, Messi had everything except for one very important thing: height. Yes, at the age of ten, Leo was still so little that his parents decided to take him to see a doctor. It turned out that Leo's body wasn't producing enough of a certain growth hormone. The good news was that there were injections that could help him grow. But the bad news? Those injections were too expensive for Leo's family, and Newell's couldn't afford them either.

Leo's family came up with a dramatic solution: to travel across the world to Barcelona, Spain, to one of the most prestigious (and wealthiest) soccer clubs in the world. When the Barcelona academy coaches saw Leo play, they were blown away by his talent. The club's technical director was so desperate to sign him that he quickly scribbled down a contract on a napkin. Done deal! Leo was a Barcelona player now, and not only that, but the club also agreed to pay for his pricey growth hormone treatment! The whole family moved to Spain to help Leo achieve his dream.

When Leo first arrived at La Masia, Barcelona's academy, aged thirteen, he struggled to settle in. But as he grew older (and taller!), his soccer talent shone through. By sixteen, he was training with the Barcelona first team and impressing everyone, including the club's Brazilian superstar, Ronaldinho. "I've just finished training with someone who is going to be better than me," the star famously said.

In 2004, Leo made his Spanish league debut for Barcelona, becoming their youngest-ever senior player at just seventeen. Seven months later, he became Barcelona's youngest-ever goal-scorer too.

As Ronaldinho lifted Leo onto his back and carried him around the stadium, a new star was born. And that was just the beginning. As the seasons went by, Leo got better and better, and so did his goals.

MESSI'S BREAKTHROUGH MOMENT

BARCELONA 5 | 2 GETAFE

APRIL 18, 2007

Leo started wide on the right wing, just inside his own half—that doesn't sound that dangerous, does it? Then again, this is "The Little Magician" we're talking about!

In a flash, Leo danced past one opponent, then nutmegged the next. As he approached the Getafe penalty area, two defenders stood in his way, but with two quick taps of the ball and a beautiful body swerve, he skipped right through them. Surely now it was time to shoot? No, Leo decided to dribble around the goalkeeper too, before sliding the ball into the empty net with his right foot.

WHOA, what a wondergoal! No one had seen anything like it since Maradona himself, against England at the 1986 World Cup. This was a player who was determined to prove himself. And the rest is soccer history . . .

MESSI'S CAREER TIMELINE

– 2009 Under new manager Pep Guardiola, Leo wins the treble with Barcelona: the Spanish league, the Spanish Cup, and the Champions League. Oh, and he also wins the Ballon d'Or (one of the most prestigious individual awards in soccer) for the first time.

– 2011 Leo helps Barcelona to win the Champions League yet again.

– 2012 He scores ninety-one goals in a single year, a ridiculous record that will surely never be broken.

– 2014 Messi becomes Barcelona's all-time record goal-scorer and the Spanish league's all-time top scorer too.

– 2015 He wins a second treble with Barcelona.

– 2017 Leo scores his five hundredth goal for Barcelona, with a last-minute winner against Ronaldo's Real Madrid.

– 2018 Leo becomes only the second player to reach one hundred Champions League goals. (The first? Yep, you guessed it . . . Cristiano Ronaldo!)

– 2021 After twenty-one years at Barcelona, Leo leaves to join French club PSG, and he also wins the Copa América with Argentina.

– 2022 Leo wins the first of two French league titles with PSG, and then the World Cup, leading Argentina to glory in Qatar.

– 2023 Messi sets off on one last amazing soccer adventure: to the USA to play for Inter Miami!

ORIGIN STORIES: CRISTIANO RONALDO

When Cristiano was born on the Portuguese island of Madeira, the doctor told his parents, Maria Dolores and José Dinis, that based on his weight, he could become a soccer player. When he was growing up, Cristiano's parents were often out for long hours while they worked to support their family. This left Ronaldo free to do what he wanted, and what he wanted to do was play soccer.

He kicked and kicked—balls, stones, pieces of fruit, whatever he could find. He practiced and practiced—right foot, left foot, plus lots of flicks and tricks. And he played and played on the streets of Funchal, his home city.

Cristiano loved showing off and scoring goals, but most of all, he loved to win. He was such a bad loser that his friends nicknamed him "Crybaby." At the age of six, Ronaldo was already the most competitive kid in Funchal. Soon after his eighth birthday, his father decided it was time for his son to start playing soccer for one of Madeira's proper teams—Andorinha.

At this small soccer club, Ronaldo had to learn a lot about tactics and teamwork, but once he had settled in, he soon became their star player. After a few amazing years, Cristiano joined Nacional, one of Madeira's most successful clubs. Then, aged twelve, he was offered an even bigger move: to Sporting Lisbon, one of the most famous soccer teams in the whole of Portugal.

Leaving behind calm island life for the chaos of Portugal's capital city, Cristiano—like Leo—left home at an early age to pursue his soccer dream. But Cristiano didn't have his family there to support him—they had to stay behind to work in Funchal. Cristiano struggled at first, but thanks to lots of support from his coaches and phone calls home to his family, he stayed focused on his dream of becoming a professional soccer player.

Did you know? Cristiano used to spend so much time at the sporting academy gym that the coaches put a lock on the door. Even that didn't stop him, however; he used buckets of water as weights and worked out in the shower instead!

When Ronaldo turned fifteen, disaster struck. One of his doctors discovered that he had a heart condition. Was this the end of his soccer career? But in true GOAT style, Ronaldo refused to give up on his dream. He had surgery and was back training in record time.

By seventeen, Ronaldo was already starring in the first team's starting lineup. He also caught the eye of lots of Europe's biggest clubs. Rumor had it that the Premier League champions, Manchester United, were looking for an electric new winger to replace David Beckham. The United manager, Sir Alex Ferguson, thought Cristiano could be just the superstar for the job. First, however, they wanted to see him in action, and so they took their team to Portugal to play a preseason friendly.

This was exactly the opportunity Ronaldo had been waiting for. But how would "Crybaby" cope under such enormous pressure?

RONALDO'S BREAKTHROUGH MOMENT

SPORTING LISBON 3 | 1 MANCHESTER UNITED

AUGUST 7, 2003

Cristiano walked out onto the field, determined to put on a memorable performance against his potential new team.

United's left-back that night, John O'Shea, didn't stand a chance—and he wasn't the only one. Cristiano danced his way through the whole defense, all while showing off his full range of twists and turns, flicks and tricks. He helped to set up Sporting's first goal with a clever pass, and it was clear to see that the eighteen-year-old wonderkid was only just getting started . . .

By full time, Ferguson had done the deal. For a fee of £12 million, Madeira's young genius was moving to Manchester United!

And the rest is soccer history . . .

RONALDO'S CAREER TIMELINE

– 2004 Cristiano wins his first trophy with Manchester United, the FA Cup, scoring in the final.

– 2008 Ronaldo wins the double with Manchester United: the Premier League and the Champions League. Oh, and he also wins the Ballon d'Or for the first time.

– 2009 Cristiano signs for Spanish giants Real Madrid for £84.6 million, becoming the world's most expensive player.

– 2011 He scores the winner for Real in the Spanish Cup final versus . . . yep, Messi's Barcelona!

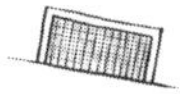

– 2014 Cristiano wins the Champions League again, scoring seventeen goals in the competition, the most ever in a single season.

– 2016 Ronaldo leads Portugal to glory at Euro 2016.

– 2017 Cristiano lifts the Champions League trophy for the fourth time, scoring two in the final against Juventus.

– 2018 Cristiano joins Juventus, where he wins two Italian league titles and becomes the first player to reach 100 Champions League goals.

– 2021 Cristiano grabs his 110th goal for Portugal, becoming the record scorer in the history of men's international soccer.

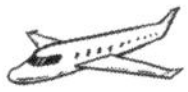

– 2022 Cristiano returns to Manchester United and breaks FIFA's all-time men's record for most goals in competitive matches.

– 2023 Cristiano sets off on one last amazing soccer adventure: to Saudi Arabia to play for Al-Nassr!

OK, so now that we've got to know our GOATs a little better, it's time to get the battle underway! But remember, this isn't going to be a wild, angry, "I'm right and you're wrong!," "You smell!" kind of battle. No, no, no—there'll be no fighting here! Instead, we're going to discuss the GOATs calmly and carefully like two soccer superfans, putting forward the best case for both players. Otherwise, it's just two people shouting at each other, and that isn't fun for anyone, is it?

Matt
We're talking good, clean fun, with no one left face down in the mud!

Seth
Think less "booo!," more "boom!"

Matt
And all "wham!" and no "slam!"

Seth
That last one was actually quite good, Matt . . . for you.

Matt
Hey, what's that supposed to mean?!

Let's kick off with Character . . .

CHARACTER

WHAT IS CHARACTER?

Don't worry, we're going to learn all about how epic Messi's and Ronaldo's skills are. But first we're going to find out about their characters. That's because skills will only get you so far as a professional soccer player.

No matter how fast you are, or how precise your shooting is, your skills will become almost worthless if you can't perform under pressure. And being a top soccer player is often very stressful. Some coaches place more importance on character than on actual skills! Even if you have incredible skills like Messi and Ronaldo, you still need character superpowers to be a GOAT.

In this section, we're going to look at . . .

PERSONALITY
We'll look at how Ronaldo and Messi get the best out of their different personalities.

MINDSET
We'll study their mindsets—ways of thinking—and how they've overcome challenges during their careers.

LEADERSHIP
We'll end by looking at how they lead and inspire the people around them.

PERSONALITY

When it comes to personality, one thing is certain—Ronaldo and Messi are *very* different. One is loud and confident, and the other is shy and humble. One shows his emotions, and the other keeps them hidden. One loves the headlines, and the other hates being spoken about. Can you guess who is who?

CRISTIANO RONALDO

We know lots about Ronaldo. We know he eats the perfect diet. He dresses well and he doesn't let a single strand of hair fall out of place. He doesn't have any tattoos and he's famous for spending as much time at the training ground as possible. And, of course, there's his iconic "*Siuuu!*" celebration—where he leaps into the air and throws his arms out wide. But what do these facts tell us about his personality?

HE'S CONFIDENT

Yes, Cristiano Ronaldo certainly loves Cristiano Ronaldo, and this GOAT loves to be the center of attention. This is the guy who in 2017, after winning his fifth Ballon d'Or, said, "I've never seen anyone better than me. I have always thought that. No soccer player can do the things I can."

WHAT THE DOUBTERS SAY

"Ronaldo is arrogant. He's only out for himself."

WRONG!

When you are arrogant, you believe that you are already the best you can be. But *confident* people understand that they can get even better if they ask for help!

Cristiano Ronaldo hasn't been afraid to ask for help time and time again in his career. Whether he's asking for support from psychologists or nutritionists, with his mental attitude or his diet, Cristiano is always on the lookout for new ways to improve. Ronaldo's confidence and self-belief ensure that he isn't afraid to try out new ideas and to push the limits of what it means to be a soccer GOAT!

HE'S DEDICATED

Ronaldo knows that to be the greatest soccer player in the world, he needs to work harder than any other soccer player in the world (*especially* Messi). As a result, he's often the first person into training and the last person to leave, staying behind to practice his free kicks, dribbling, and finishing.

When Ronaldo goes home, he takes perfect care of his body. He eats healthy food made by his personal chef to restore his energy, takes ice baths to help his aching muscles recover, works with his personal trainer to improve his strength, and checks in with his doctor to make sure his body is at its best. Even as an experienced superstar, Ronaldo still trains harder than anyone else.

HE HAS HIGH STANDARDS

Cristiano is obsessed with scoring goals. Even if his team wins the game, he's often not happy unless *he* scores. Given this, he's sometimes accused of being too much of an individual and not enough of a team player.

It's true that Ronaldo is motivated by individual achievements, but he also knows that you have to pull together as a team if you want to win big trophies! Throughout his career, Ronaldo has inspired many of his teammates with his relentless will to win. "He never wanted his standards to drop," said Manchester United coach Mike Phelan after Ronaldo joined the club for the second time in 2022. "He wanted his teammates to raise their standards instead."

So yes, Ronaldo is a bit of an individual. But he knows that to be the best, you need a bit of help from your teammates too.

LIONEL MESSI

So, what do we know about Messi? We know that he once wore a sparkly suit to the Ballon d'Or ceremony. He has lots of tattoos, including:

Other than that, however, the answer is—we don't know very much about Messi! Despite being a soccer superstar, this GOAT candidate prefers to stay out of the spotlight.

HE'S SHY

As a young Barcelona player, Messi was so shy that he used to get changed in the corridor rather than the locker room! He wanted to become the best player in the world, but the fame that went with it? No, thank you! After scoring his first goal for Barcelona, Messi told a friend, "I hate it that people are now talking about me. I hope they talk less." Messi never got his wish . . .

Being shy or reserved could be a problem in a soccer team, but with Messi it isn't a concern. That's because the one place Messi isn't shy is on the soccer field! This soccer GOAT demands the ball in difficult places, dances past defenders, and takes risks even when he could lose the ball. Messi might not be the loudest player on the field, but there are many different ways you can communicate as a soccer player. Messi spends a lot of time listening to his teammates, and he also uses strong body language during games.

HE'S CALM

No matter what's going on around him, Messi usually manages to keep his emotions under control. Even when defenders kick him, he doesn't react because he knows that being angry won't help him to perform at his best. And when he scores an incredible goal, he often stays calm and smiles. "I'm always looking to remain as calm and relaxed as possible when I go onto the field," Messi once said. "When I feel the grass beneath my feet, I feel sure, because playing soccer is what I enjoy the most."

Just like Ronaldo, Messi has supreme confidence in his abilities. This confidence allows him to perform under pressure and to score mind-blowing goals.

HE'S COMPETITIVE

Messi might have once said, "I am more concerned about being a good person than being the best soccer player in the world." But don't be fooled; when it comes to soccer, Messi is a ruthless winner who is never satisfied.

WHAT THE DOUBTERS SAY

"Messi has never had to work very hard. His soccer talent is all natural."

WRONG!

"Messi in training was very competitive," said Maso, a soccer player from the same generation at La Masia, the Barcelona academy. "He always wanted to win." And that hasn't changed at all.

The former captain of the Barcelona B team Arnau Riera remembers Messi crying one day after a devastating 4–1 defeat to Zaragoza B. "That surprised me, because I didn't think losing would hurt him," Arnau reportedly said. Messi might have plenty of natural talent, but it is his dedication and competitive nature that drive him to be the best he can be.

Free kicks, penalties, shots, passes, and dribbles all require hours and hours of practice, even if your name is Lionel Messi! And for the greatest soccer players, that practice never stops. When Messi scored his first goal for the Barcelona first team in 2004, and the soccer world went wild, Messi responded by calmly saying, "I start early and I stay late, day after day, year after year. It took me seventeen years and a hundred and fourteen days to become an overnight success."

WHO'S THE WINNER?

Confident v. quiet. Emotional v. calm. Ronaldo and Messi have *very* different personalities, but that doesn't mean that one is better than the other! The most important thing is that both players have found ways to get the best out of themselves.

Interestingly, our GOATs aren't different in every department. In fact, their MINDSETS are scarily similar—let's look at them next.

MINDSET

A person's mindset is their way of thinking and their attitude toward life. A positive mindset is especially important when things don't go according to plan.

WHAT THE DOUBTERS SAY

"Messi and Ronaldo have had it easy! They're super successful, and nothing has ever gone wrong for them!"

WRONG!

Our GOATs haven't always enjoyed success. In fact, they've both had a lot go wrong during their careers. They've been told they're not good enough, been booed by their own fans, missed super-important penalties, and even failed in big finals. But what makes Messi and Ronaldo so great is that they've overcome these obstacles in style. They both have positive mindsets that allow them to keep going when times get tough.

As young players starting out, Messi and Ronaldo had to learn how to face challenges head-on.

Leaving home at such an early age must have been difficult, but our GOATs were determined to follow their dreams. Even when Ronaldo was having a tough time at the Sporting Lisbon academy, he didn't give up. He repeated the same words to everyone around him: "I'm going to become the best soccer player in the world."

These soccer superstars are never satisfied. "I never saw a player as demanding of himself," Messi's Barcelona coach Tito Vilanova reportedly said. "Sometimes he would play a fantastic game but then leave the field angry with himself because he thought he could have done better."

As they grew into the best soccer players in the world, our GOATs also became each other's motivation. If Ronaldo scored a hat trick one week, Messi would somehow score four goals the week after. If Messi nutmegged three defenders, Ronaldo would want to nutmeg four! With such competition, both players pushed each other to grow and to become the best they could possibly be.

There have been plenty of obstacles for our GOATs to overcome over the years. So, let's see those positive mindsets in action . . .

LIONEL MESSI: FROM PENALTY PAIN TO WORLD CUP JOY

It's the 2016 Copa América final, Argentina v. Chile. Messi is about to take a penalty that could help end twenty-three years of pain.

Argentina has been runner-up in three of the last four Copa América tournaments, and runner-up in the last World Cup too. But now Messi has the opportunity to win a final for Argentina. Messi steps up and—oh no!—he blasts it over the bar! Disaster!

After the game, Messi cried and cried. Argentina was relying on him to win a trophy, like their all-time hero, Diego Maradona, had at the 1986 World Cup. But for the fourth time, Messi's team had fallen at the final hurdle. "He's lazy. He's a lie! He's no Maradona!" the fans roared.

A SHOCK FOR THE WORLD OF SOCCER

After the game, Messi made an announcement: "The victory was the thing I wanted the most, but I couldn't get it. So I think

it's over." Whoa, what? How could *Lionel Messi* retire from international soccer?

But the more Messi thought about it, the more he realized that quitting wasn't the right thing to do. Sure, he'd experienced lots of setbacks with Argentina, but he loved playing for his country. And just because Argentina had lost so many finals, it didn't mean they couldn't win one again in the future . . .

Messi was determined to win a trophy for his country, and two years later his team returned for the 2018 World Cup. Although Argentina lost to France in the Round of Sixteen, there was no doubt that the team's performances were improving. And at the 2021 Copa América, Messi's hard work finally paid off. Argentina beat Brazil in the final and they won a trophy at last! And who won the Ballon d'Or and Player of the Tournament award (with four goals and five assists)? You've guessed it: Messi!

By the time Argentina arrived at the 2022 World Cup, they were unbeaten in thirty-six games.

COULD THIS BE ARGENTINA'S TOURNAMENT?

Messi was like a man possessed—playing some of the most incredible soccer of his career:

- He scored the first goal and set up the second when Argentina beat Mexico in the group stage.
- In the Round of Sixteen, he coolly rolled the ball through an Australian defender's legs and around the keeper.
- In the quarterfinals, he set up Nahuel Molina's goal with a sublime, defense-splitting pass.
- In the semifinals, he twisted past Croatian defender Joško Gvardiol, before pulling the ball back for Julián Álvarez to score.

THE BEST WAS YET TO COME

Messi saved his biggest performance of all for the final against France. Messi scored from the penalty spot, and his goal was quickly followed by a superb strike from Ángel Di María. It was 2–0 to Argentina! Things were looking very promising for Messi's team.

But just when it looked like it was game over, French player Kylian Mbappé came alive, making it 2–1, then 2–2. The question was: Could Messi hold his nerve?

When the match went to penalties, Messi stepped up first for Argentina and . . . SCORED! Six spot kicks later, it was all over and Argentina was the new World Champion!

If Messi had believed his critics back in 2016, he would have quit international soccer for good. Instead, he bounced back from his setbacks and proved to the Argentinians that he was just as good as Diego Maradona—maybe even better. ■

CRISTIANO RONALDO: FROM WINKER TO WINNER

Flashback to 2006: Cristiano Ronaldo is a rising star at Manchester United. But he's also the most-hated soccer player in England.

Why? For winking. No, seriously. For winking. 😉

In the 2006 World Cup quarterfinals, England played against Portugal. With the score at 0–0, England's Wayne Rooney caused outrage by stepping on Portugal's Ricardo Carvalho. Led by Ronaldo, Portugal's players immediately swarmed the referee and demanded a red card. "He didn't even touch him, ref!" the England players argued. But the referee showed Rooney a red card, and as his Manchester United treammate stormed off the field, the TV cameras zoomed in on Ronaldo—who winked!

THE FINAL STRAW

Boooo! That wink was the final straw for England's distraught fans. After the game, newspapers printed furious headlines about Ronaldo, with one even saying, "Don't let this man into our country any more!" Ronaldo had made himself public enemy number one—just in time for the start of the Premier League.

"When I arrived back in England, I was kind of afraid," Ronaldo later said. "Not because of Rooney, but because of the England supporters."

At first, every time he touched the ball, Ronaldo was booed—even by the Manchester United supporters! In that hateful atmosphere, many players would have tried to hide, but not Cristiano. "He'll never be frightened to show his ability because he's got great courage," said Manchester United manager Sir Alex Ferguson.

He was right: Ronaldo saw the reaction as another challenge to overcome. "It's not nice to be booed in every stadium, but some good can come of it," Ronaldo said later. "It makes you stronger psychologically."

Ignoring the noise, Ronaldo focused on being the best soccer player he could be. From scoring eleven goals in the previous season, Ronaldo jumped to twenty-three. Before long, the boos from the crowd were gradually replaced by cheers. Ronaldo had successfully earned the crowd's respect, and that wasn't all. With Wayne Rooney alongside him in attack, Manchester United soon lifted the Premier League title.

The winker had bounced back to become a winner. ■

WHO'S THE WINNER?

So, there you have it—just two of the many stories that show the power of Messi's and Ronaldo's mindsets. Their personalities may be total opposites, but their mindsets are incredibly similar. Neither will rest until he is the best possible version of himself, which often inspires the players around them to aim for the same. This leads us nicely on to LEADERSHIP.

LEADERSHIP

Being able to lead and inspire others is an essential quality when it comes to being a GOAT. The more united and motivated your teammates are, the more likely they are to play well.

Although Messi and Ronaldo are strong characters, leadership probably isn't the first quality that comes to mind when you think of these GOATs. In fact, some soccer fans think they both played their best club soccer while teammates such as Carles Puyol and Sergio Ramos wore the captain's armband! Puyol and Ramos were arguably better suited to captaincy at the time—more encouraging, more selfless, and better communicators.

But as Messi and Ronaldo became more experienced, their influence grew. Before long, they were asked to wear the armband for their national teams—Ronaldo in 2008 (aged twenty-three) and Messi in 2011 (aged twenty-four). Did that make them fantastic leaders? Not straightaway, no. But as we've already seen in this section, these soccer GOATs believe that they can always improve.

LIONEL MESSI

WHAT THE DOUBTERS SAY

"Messi will never be a leader. . . . He's scared."
Diego Maradona, Argentina legend and former captain, 2011

WRONG!

It is a common mistake to think that all captains have to be loud and command their teammates. Actually, there are many different ways to lead effectively. In Messi's case, he often leads by example—demanding the ball and inspiring others with his incredible skills. Still, criticism after a bad run of results for Argentina in 2011 made Messi look at ways he could improve as a leader. Communication, he decided, was key.

Leading the motivational pre-match talk to the team didn't come easily to Messi, but the more he did it, the easier it became to express his emotions. And during the 2021 Copa América final, Messi's improved leadership skills were rewarded. In his pre-match talk, Messi "lost his mind" according to teammate Ángel Di María. Shy little Messi was transformed into a passionate and inspiring leader, willing his team on to victory. As we know, it was this final when Argentina won a major trophy after years of waiting. When the whistle blew, the players all ran to their leader to celebrate. And Messi wasn't done yet!

After a surprise defeat against Saudi Arabia in the opening game of the 2022 World Cup, Argentina needed a leader more than ever. To keep their spirits up, Messi called his team together and promised them that if they worked hard then they would still qualify. Then he spoke directly to the Argentinian fans: "Believe in us. We won't let you down." Deal! The supporters stuck with their team, and Argentina didn't let them down. Suddenly, Messi was in the form of his life, stepping up with match-winning moments and securing Argentina a spot in the final.

When the final went all the way to a penalty shoot-out, Argentina needed someone to step up. Leaders can't be scared in such high-pressure situations, and Messi certainly wasn't. He took the first penalty—GOAL!

Messi might not be a natural public speaker, but this soccer GOAT's actions showed that there are many different ways that you can be a great leader.

CRISTIANO RONALDO

Like Messi, Ronaldo is also a captain who prefers to lead by example on the field. On one famous occasion, however, he was forced to adapt and become a leader from the sidelines . . .

In 2016, Portugal reached the final in the European Championship, or Euros, where they faced France, the tournament hosts and favorites. Ronaldo knew that his team was relying on him to be their superstar, but ten minutes into the game, disaster struck. *CRUNCH!* A tackle from Dimitri Payet left him rolling around in agony. Ronaldo tried to play on, but after twenty-three minutes he had to leave the field on a stretcher. What was Portugal going to do without their leader? In the locker room, Ronaldo cried and cried. He had desperately wanted to win the trophy for his country, and now he couldn't. Or could he?

With the game still going on, Ronaldo suddenly realized he could help! At halftime, he told his teammates: "I'm sure we will win, so stay together and fight for it." Then, as the second half started, he stood beside his manager, shouting instructions like a coach.

In the seventy-ninth minute, Portugal's sub striker, Eder, ran onto the field with an inspiring message from Ronaldo ringing in his ears: "You're going to score." And that's exactly what happened. In the 109th minute, Eder hit a rocket of a shot, which cannoned into France's goal. 1–0!

Ronaldo charged about on the sidelines. His knee hurt, but he didn't care. When the final whistle blew, he was in the middle of all the celebrations. Together, they had done it; they were the Champions of Europe! After that devastating injury, it would have been easy for Ronaldo to sit and sulk—he loved being the hero. But like all great leaders, he realized that the team was more important than he was. With their star player urging them on from the sidelines, Portugal had played with extra desire and belief.

WHO'S THE WINNER?

Leadership may not be the first thing that comes to mind when you think of Messi or Ronaldo, but that doesn't mean it isn't a strength of theirs. Although they may not have been natural captains to start with, through years of hard work each has become a successful leader in his own way.

SO COME ON THEN . . . WHO IS THE CHARACTER GOAT?

In the Character section, we've looked at what our GOATs are like as people, players, and leaders. Now it's over to Matt to make the case for Messi.

MATT'S CASE FOR MESSI

We all know that Messi was born with a special gift, but it takes more than just talent to become the best soccer player in the world and stay there for more than ten years. Just ask Ronaldinho or Allan Simonsen. (Who? Exactly!) You need huge amounts of dedication and determination, and when it comes to character, Messi is the absolute master of both.

First, let's talk dedication. Behind the scenes and behind that shy personality, Messi is the ultimate pro, working hard every day to improve. That free kick against Liverpool in the 2018–19 Champions League, that twist and turn past Joško Gvardiol in the 2022 World Cup—those skills take hours of practice, even if your name is Lionel Messi.

Next up: determination. As part of Pep Guardiola's successful Barcelona team, Messi hasn't had to deal with too many disappointments over his career, but for Argentina, he has had to handle pressure like no other player ever. You try being "the next Maradona," expected to lead your country to the World Cup trophy! It's no surprise that for years, Messi's international career was a story of failure. But when he decided to give up in 2016, he soon came roaring back, more determined than ever.

At the 2022 World Cup, Messi was the same amazing player, but he was a different kind of leader, showing a lot more personality and passion. And look what happened—he finally won the trophy for Argentina!

So, let me do the math for you: talent + dedication + determination + leadership = Messi is the soccer GOAT!

SETH'S CASE FOR RONALDO

Ronaldo doesn't just want to be the greatest soccer player of all time. He wants to be perfect. But being perfect isn't always easy. Living a life as a professional soccer player will test even the strongest of characters. For instance, having to move away from your entire family to live in a strange city, or having the whole of England hate you just because you winked! But Ronaldo is also a player who thrives under pressure. Which is why when the crowds in England booed him, he focused on his performances and let his feet do the talking. Soon, those same crowds couldn't help but applaud.

There's a reason that Cristiano is so confident. His commitment to soccer is unrivaled. Even if he was born with a God-given talent, he's worked hard for every trophy. His buckets of sweat transformed into sweet success, and soon the records and awards piled up.

No matter how much he achieves, Cristiano always wants more. He never settles for second best and he always aims high. He didn't just want one Champions League—he wanted five.

He didn't just want forty goals in a season—he wanted to break every goal-scoring record that ever stood!

Ronaldo makes the impossible possible. Portugal had never won a major international trophy before Cristiano was handed the captain's armband (aged just twenty-three!). Thanks to his leadership, they now have a Nations League *and* a European Championship! Ronaldo isn't just a mentality monster—he's the true soccer GOAT.

Matt
A "mentality monster"? More like an "ego ogre" if you ask me!

Seth
I didn't ask you!

Matt
Well, you kind of did, since we're writing this book together.

Seth
I'm starting to regret that, mate!

THE SCORES ARE IN:

	MESSI	RONALDO
PERSONALITY RATING	9/10	9/10
MINDSET RATING	9/10	10/10
LEADERSHIP RATING	8/10	8/10
TOTAL SCORE	26/30	27/30

So, that's what we think, but we're not the real decision-makers here—*you* are! Who do you think is the Character GOAT and why?

My Character GOAT is

. . . .

SKILLS

WHAT ARE SKILLS?

As well as having totally different personalities, Messi and Ronaldo also showcase very different *skills* on the soccer field. One is super speedy, while the other is amazingly agile. One hammers the ball as hard as he can, while the other carefully places it into the net. One loves a stepover; the other favors a nutmeg.

When you hear the word *skills*, you may think of fancy soccer tricks like flip-flaps and around-the-worlds. But in reality, soccer skills are so much more than that. We're going to break this section down into three key areas:

PHYSICAL SKILLS
We're talking speed, strength, and power.

TECHNICAL SKILLS
We'll analyze Messi's and Ronaldo's technical skills—dribbling, passing, and shooting.

TACTICAL SKILLS
Finally, we'll look at how our GOATs use tactical skills to influence their games.

PHYSICAL SKILLS

You can have the maddest technical skills ever, but you also need incredible physical skills to be a soccer GOAT. As professional soccer players, Messi and Ronaldo know that they need to train their bodies to be as strong, quick, and powerful as possible. They need:

- The strength to hold off challenges
- The speed to get away from opponents
- The power to unleash long-range shots on goal

CRISTIANO RONALDO

Ronaldo may have started his career as a skinny teenager, but his work in the gym has transformed his body! If you look at Ronaldo today, you'd think he's the perfect athlete. He has the long limbs of a high jumper, the muscular legs of a sprinter, and the lean body of a long-distance runner. But what are his top physical skills?

HE'S STRONG

Cristiano Ronaldo is pure muscle. He uses his incredible strength to outjump opponents for headers, outmuscle defenders, and shoot with super force. In his first season at Manchester United, Ronaldo won 40 percent of his battles in the air with defenders. This was an impressive statistic, but we know that Ronaldo is always looking for ways to improve! Cristiano dedicated himself to training in the gym, and he soon became so strong that he could hold off defenders with ease. By his second season at Manchester United, Ronaldo was winning 66 percent of his aerial duels.

Did you know? Ronaldo's Real Madrid teammates nicknamed him La Máquina: The Machine!

HE'S FAST

Ronaldo is lethal at his top speed, and it's very difficult for defenders to catch him once this GOAT gets going. Yes, Ronaldo truly is a speed demon. At the 2018 World Cup, FIFA clocked Ronaldo's top speed at 21 mph (34 kph), while Messi only registered at 20 mph (32.5 kph). Ronaldo was an incredible 1 mph (1.5 kph) quicker than Messi! Ronaldo's rapid pace means he's famous for launching counterattacks at a moment's notice—when his team intercepts the ball, he speeds away without giving his opponents time to think or to get organized!

HE'S POWERFUL

When you combine speed and strength, you get power. And there are very few soccer players who are more powerful than Ronaldo. His shots explode from his right foot at speeds of over 80 mph (129 kph)! When Ronaldo jumps, he generates so much power that he has been known to leap 3½ ft (1.06 m) off the ground—that's 2¾ in (7 cm) higher than the average jump of a professional basketball player! And when

Ronaldo goes up, he doesn't come straight back down. When playing for Juventus in 2019, Ronaldo hung in the air for an incredible 1.5 seconds before powering a header past the goalkeeper!

LIONEL MESSI

Lionel Messi isn't tall, and he isn't particularly muscular, either. He isn't naturally suited to charging around the soccer field like Ronaldo—in fact, he spends most of his time walking. But while Ronaldo's greater height and weight allow him to perform better in some areas, Messi's size and shape help him in others . . .

HE'S AGILE

Most soccer players rarely get up to their top speeds during games—pesky defenders do their best to get in the way of the ball. Attackers like Messi and Ronaldo often have to twist, turn, and break away in order to score. This is where Messi's physical disadvantages become his greatest advantages. Messi's shorter figure gives him a low center of gravity, which means he's much more agile (able to move quickly and easily) than your average soccer player. While taller players like Ronaldo would have to slow down and take smaller strides while dribbling, Messi's height means he can weave past defenders and accelerate away from them at close to top speed. Speedy Ronaldo would beat Messi in a 100-meter race, but Messi would almost certainly win in an agility test!

HE'S SURPRISINGLY STRONG

When you think of strength, you don't necessarily think of Lionel Messi. He certainly doesn't have Ronaldo's muscles, and he can't lift as much weight or shoot with as much force.

WHAT THE DOUBTERS SAY

> "Messi was successful in the Spanish league, where the pace is slower and there's more passing. But in a faster, more physical league like the Premier League he'd be too weak."
>
> **WRONG!**

Fast. Furious. Physical. There are few matches in the world more demanding than El Clásico (Real Madrid v. Barcelona). The Spanish League's most competitive match is played at incredible intensity. Long story short: It isn't a game for the weak. Which is exactly why Messi dominated so many matches against Real Madrid.

The little Argentinian might not be the biggest attacker around, but he doesn't need to be. Due to his short build, defenders find that he has a surprisingly strong base that is near impossible to break. Watch any El Clásico games and you'll see Real Madrid players desperately trying to pull Messi back as he accelerates away from them. He is an expert at protecting the ball with his body—getting his butt and hips in the way of defenders so they'll be forced to foul him if they try to get the ball.

HE'S GOT GREAT BALANCE

Messi's surprising strength is aided by his brilliant balance. His short build and low center of gravity mean he is easily able to adjust himself as he moves around the field. This soccer GOAT twists and turns as he runs, staying low to the ground and using his arms to hold himself steady. Whether he's weaving past defenders or sprinting toward the ball, Messi's impressive balancing skills mean he is always able to keep moving at a rapid pace. Take his "goal of the century" against Getafe. Messi effortlessly shifted the ball from left to right, keeping his balance as he moved past defenders (all five of them!), who did their best to take chunks out of his legs! He evaded three slide tackles and remained on his feet even under intense physical pressure. With such agility, strength, and balance, no Getafe player even came close to stopping Messi!

WHO'S THE WINNER?

Ronaldo is undoubtedly stronger and more powerful than Messi. But while Ronaldo can outmuscle opponents, Messi can twist and turn away from them. Ronaldo might win the GOAT debate when it comes to physical skills, but Messi is proof that physical skills are not everything.

TECHNICAL SKILLS

When Messi and Ronaldo get the ball, fans hold their breath and defenders panic and do everything in their power to try and stop our GOATs. Control, pass, dribble, shoot: Messi and Ronaldo can do it all. But who has the ultimate technical skills?

CRISTIANO RONALDO

DRIBBLING

When Ronaldo started out as a professional soccer player, he had such a big box of tricks that at times it felt like he was about to pull a rabbit out of his cleats! From sensational stepovers to chops and rolls, Ronaldo loved nothing more than fooling defenders. This soccer GOAT was famous for using short, quick touches to draw defenders in, beat them with a skill (usually a stepover—or five), and then speed away. In 2004–05, Ronaldo attempted on average a whopping 9.55 dribbles per match!

But as Ronaldo has gotten older, his strategy has shifted and he's become much more focused on scoring goals. At Manchester United in 2005,

Ronaldo's coaches made the groundbreaking decision to adjust his position. They moved him closer to the opponents' goal, where he had more chances to shoot. Ronaldo has gone on to become one of the best goal-scorers in the world, but his role as a striker has meant that he has less need to dribble. Ronaldo does still pull out his bag of tricks when they're required, though—during his final season at Juventus, his dribbling success rate was an incredible 62 percent!

PASSING

Yes, Ronaldo is famous for his impressive scoring record, but that doesn't mean he isn't also capable of amazing passes! Although Messi is often considered the master of passing, Ronaldo has also created his share of incredible goals over the years:

	RONALDO	MESSI
KEY PASSES	890	1,387
BIG CHANCES CREATED	176	408
ASSISTS	312	439

WHAT THE DOUBTERS SAY

"Ronaldo plays for himself. He doesn't even know how to pass!"

WRONG!

Ronaldo's numbers prove that this statement is simply not true! In fact, some of Ronaldo's greatest moments have come from passes. Think about that backheel assist for Karim Benzema in Real Madrid's 3–0 win over Granada in 2014, that thirty-yard flick for Wayne Rooney in 2008 that took out Aston Villa's entire defense, or the 2014 overhead kick assist against Real Betis. Sometimes it seems as if Ronaldo has eyes in the back of his head!

And Messi hasn't always been the superior passer. In 2012–13, Ronaldo played more key passes (86) than Messi (63) and he created more chances for his team (18 compared to 13). But as Ronaldo's position has moved closer to the goal, he has had less need to pass—and more opportunity to shoot!

SHOOTING

Early in his career, Ronaldo developed a reputation for long-range shots. There were screamers against Arsenal and Portsmouth, and a forty-yard strike against Porto that earned him the 2009 FIFA Puskás Award, which is given for the world's "most beautiful" goal of the year. Ronaldo's shooting success continued at Real Madrid, where he took more shots than any other player in Europe in every single season! Given Ronaldo's immense power, it's no surprise that he loves to shoot from long range. But this soccer GOAT is also deadly up close. Ronaldo may favor his right foot, but he can score goals with his left foot and his head. Put simply, he can create goal-scoring opportunities from anywhere . . .

LIONEL MESSI

DRIBBLING

Lionel Messi is known as the master of dribbling. While Ronaldo often uses dramatic skills to fool opponents, Messi moves the ball with simple, quick steps: "I wait for the defender's movement. I play with him. Once I see what he does, I feint to go one way then go the other," Messi explained. Messi is so good at recognizing when defenders are off-balance that he is almost always able to choose the perfect moment to glide past them. It's as if the ball is glued to his foot! In 2007–08, Messi managed more successful dribbles than

Ronaldo for the first time (168 v. 128)—and the records have stayed that way ever since.

PASSING

As we've seen, Messi's passing figures are on a different planet! While Ronaldo moved closer to the goal as he got older, Messi has moved farther back. This soccer GOAT scans the field like a hawk, then picks out a defense-splitting pass that nobody else has seen.

Messi is not only a master of disguising passes from defenders, but also of timing and playing them perfectly. He loves a one-two to create space or to play an incredible pass from deep inside the opponents' half. Take his reverse pass through Nathan Aké's legs against the Netherlands in the 2022 World Cup, his dink for Thierry Henry in Barcelona's 6–2 thrashing of Real Madrid, or that flick for Neymar Jr as PSG beat Clermont Foot 5–0 . . . he's a genius!

SHOOTING

When Messi's not setting up goals for his teammates, he's usually scoring them!

WHAT THE DOUBTERS SAY

"Ronaldo is a more natural goal-scorer than Messi. His finishing is way more clinical."

WRONG!

Well, let's take a look at the numbers:

	MESSI	RONALDO
GOALS PER GAME	0.79	0.72
SHOTS PER GOAL	5.27	6.43
MINUTES PER GOAL	104.7	112.8

Yes, when it comes to scoring goals, Messi actually takes fewer shots and fewer minutes to find the net. While Ronaldo is known for his long-range shots, Messi has actually scored more goals from outside the area (92 compared to 76). Ronaldo goes for power, whereas Messi favors precision. Messi tends to shoot when he's more likely to score, while Ronaldo likes to try his luck at tricky shots from a long distance.

Did you know? During the period that both superstars played in Spain's La Liga, Ronaldo took 618 more shots than Messi, but Messi scored twenty-two more goals!

From inside the area, Messi is just as deadly. He loves to play a game of cat and mouse, waiting for the goalkeeper to make a move before choosing which shot to use. He usually favors his magic left foot.

WHO'S THE WINNER?

Ronaldo combines his physical advantages with technical skills to devastating effect. Time and time again, he leaves crowds saying "Wow!" But Messi leaves crowds asking "How?!" The Little Magician combines technical skills with expert tactics to create soccer moments that are truly out of this world.

TACTICAL SKILLS

When you hear the word *tactics*, you may well think of formations such as 4-4-2 or 3-4-1-2. And yes, those are tactics, but they're not necessarily the tactical skills we're going to judge our GOATs by! We're most interested in how Messi and Ronaldo decide which skills to use, when to use them, and how those skills affect their teammates. So, who do you think has the ultimate soccer brain?

CRISTIANO RONALDO

When Ronaldo steps onto a field, he is often able to predict what is about to happen before it does. He's practiced so much that he can use his experience to work out how defenders will react, where his teammates will move, and where the perfect space on the field will be.

In the documentary *Tested to the Limit*, director Mike McDowall set out to show how incredible Ronaldo's soccer brain is. The film crew created an experiment where they asked someone to cross a ball to Ronaldo, who then had to shoot into an empty net. Easy enough, right? But what if the lights went out? Now that sounds like a challenge! To prove how difficult this was, the crew asked an amateur soccer player to have a go first. As expected, the amateur soccer player missed the ball by a long way! Ronaldo, meanwhile, scored the first time—and again the second time. During the documentary, the crew explained how Ronaldo had analyzed the body position of the crosser, noticed the shape of their feet and hips, and predicted exactly where and when the ball would land.

Ronaldo is so experienced that he's able to make quick strategic decisions with very little information. Take his overhead kick for Real Madrid against Juventus in the Champions League in 2018. In a matter of seconds, Ronaldo had to work out where the space was, where the ball was likely to land, which shot to use, which direction the goalkeeper was moving in—and where to aim. Phew!

LIONEL MESSI

During a soccer match, Messi's brain is constantly whirring—even if it may not look like he's doing very much! At the 2022 World Cup, Messi only traveled an average of $3\frac{1}{8}$ miles (5.1 km) per game, and he walked more than any other player. Messi isn't walking because he's tired or lazy, though. This soccer GOAT is waiting for the perfect moment to strike—he's analyzing where his opponents are, what they're doing, and where the space is.

Messi's soccer brain is often working overtime to anticipate what is about to happen. Take his assist for Argentina against the Netherlands in the 2022 World Cup. In a matter of seconds, Messi had to shake off a defender, look up to see where his teammates were, decide whether to pass or dribble—and place his pass exactly where the defender couldn't stop it!

Our GOATs weren't born with these brilliant decision-making skills; they've both had to learn a lot of tough lessons over the years. Natural talent can only take you so far in professional soccer, and Messi and Ronaldo have had to *adapt* to become the superstars they are today.

Let's look at a couple of examples . . .

CRISTIANO RONALDO: FROM FLASHY FOOTWORK TO GOLDEN BOOTS

When Ronaldo arrived at Manchester United, there was no doubt that he had the talent to become a superstar. But how would he cope with the more direct, physical style of English soccer? The answer was: not very well.

Cristiano kept trying too many skills, instead of shooting or setting up his teammates. "Pass it!" everyone shouted, but he didn't seem to listen, and when defenders went to tackle him, he often dived on the ground. How frustrating!

But with the help of his Manchester United coaches, Ronaldo adapted his game: from flicks and tricks to crosses and shots, from a flashy winger to a powerful, world-class forward!

Season after season, Ronaldo got better and better. He scored six goals in 2003–04, nine goals in 2004–05, and twelve goals in 2005–06. By 2006–07, he was scoring twenty-three goals per season! And he wasn't done yet . . .

Ronaldo was desperate to keep on adapting and improving, especially when the United coach René Meulensteen challenged him to score thirty goals in the 2007–08 season! "You're good at scoring beautiful goals from long range with your right foot," Meulensteen told him, "but what about goals from close range with the rest of your body?"

Challenge accepted! Ronaldo worked hard to become more direct and much more physical in his goal-scoring. In February 2008, he reached his original target of thirty goals—all scored in very different ways. By the end of the season he had forty-two goals! Mission accomplished!

RONALDO'S GOALS, 2007–08

RIGHT FOOT	LEFT FOOT	HEADERS
26	7	9

Cristiano has carried on developing his game throughout his career. He has successfully adapted to teams with very different styles, different managers, and different teammates in the Premier League, La Liga, Serie A, and Saudi Pro League. What a superstar! ■

LET'S LOOK AT HOW RONALDO HAS ADAPTED HIS GAME OVER THE YEARS

Ronaldo has adapted from a striker in the Sporting Lisbon youth teams . . .

to a winger in the Sporting Lisbon first team . . .

to becoming much more focused on goal-scoring at Manchester United . . .

to developing into a dynamic forward at Real Madrid . . .

to becoming a superb finisher at Juventus, Manchester United, and Al-Nassr.

LIONEL MESSI: FROM BALL HOG TO BALLONS D'OR

For all his magical talents, young Leo had a lot to learn when it came to team play.

"He's too selfish," cried his Barcelona B teammates. "And he doesn't defend when he loses the ball." If Leo was ever going to succeed he'd have to—yep you guessed it—adapt his game!

Messi's Barcelona B coach was the first to talk to him: "The game carries on if you don't have the ball," he said. "And sometimes your teammates are in better positions than you."

Leo worked hard to impress his coach. He buzzed around the field and improved his passing so much that he got called into the first team.

BECOMING THE ULTIMATE TEAM PLAYER

Under Pep Guardiola, Messi finally learned to pass to his teammates and how to tackle. "I think Messi is the one who wins the ball back the most when he loses possession," said former Liverpool manager Jürgen Klopp. And when he did win the ball, Messi was always willing to pass

to the player in the best position. Messi had shown his impressive ability to adapt. Sometimes Pep played Messi on the wing, other times as a forward, a "false nine" (a striker who drops into midfield to build play), or even as an attacking midfielder. Often Messi would perform all those roles in a single game!

THE "MSN" ERA

With his teammates Suárez and Neymar, Messi went on to form a much-feared attack known as "MSN." In three seasons, the teammates scored 363 goals between them (Messi scored 153 of them)! Along the way, Messi also picked up heaps of individual awards, but even though the spotlight was on him, he knew that he wouldn't have succeeded without the support of his teammates and coaches.

When Messi won the 2010 Ballon d'Or, he recognized his support from teammates Xavi and Andrés Iniesta that season: "I want to make a toast to Xavi and Andrés," Messi said. "Despite the fact that I won, they deserve the award—this is for them." ■

LET'S LOOK AT HOW MESSI HAS ADAPTED HIS GAME OVER THE YEARS

Messi adapted from playing as a winger in Barcelona's youth team . . .

to working with Xavi and Iniesta in the first team . . .

to floating around the front three as part of the legendary "MSN" formation . . .

to having the entire Barcelona team built around him . . .

to dropping deeper to create as he got older, particularly at PSG and the 2022 World Cup . . .

to a free role at Inter Miami—operating both in central attacking positions and in wider positions on the wings.

WHO'S THE WINNER?

Messi and Ronaldo might be two of the sharpest minds in the history of soccer, but neither one of them thinks they know it all. It's clear to see that these GOATs are always happy to adapt and make changes to their game to suit the team.

What separates Messi on tactical skills, however, is his incredible speed of thought that allows him to see games in slow motion and make the right decisions in the right moments. While Ronaldo's mind is sharper than sharp, even Seth can admit that Messi has the ultimate tactical brain!

SO COME ON THEN . . . WHO IS THE SKILLS GOAT?

In this Skills section, we've looked at Messi and Ronaldo's physical, technical, and tactical skills. Now it's time to take what we've discussed and VOTE FOR THE GOAT!

Over to Matt to make the case for the wing wizard turned central creator . . .

MATT'S CASE FOR MESSI

When it comes to soccer skills, Messi is the GOAT, no doubt about it. The guy is so good that he doesn't even need to use any flip-flaps or rainbow flicks. No, he just gets the ball and glides past top defenders (Jérôme Boateng, Joško Gvardiol—the list goes on and on) like they're clumsy giants with flippers instead of feet!

Passing, dribbling, shooting—Messi is the absolute master of all three, and he makes it look so effortless and easy. He really is the soccer player that puts the "beautiful" in "the beautiful game."

No, Messi isn't a physical beast like Ronaldo, but so what? He's a lot stronger than he looks, and his soccer brain is so powerful and fast that he doesn't need to have a show-off six-pack. Even under big-game pressure, he somehow still sees things that no one else has spotted—a teeny-tiny gap in the defense, a teammate about to run, an opponent slightly off balance—and then he has the skills to take full advantage.

Don't be fooled into believing Messi's lazy just because he walks around a lot. He's always thinking and watching for an opportunity. And don't be fooled into thinking Messi just does whatever he wants on the field. He's a team player as well as a superstar, and he has adapted his game again and again to suit the talents around him. But come on—if you had the GOAT on your team, would you really want to waste his talent by asking him to track back and defend? Exactly!

SETH'S CASE FOR RONALDO

In his prime, no soccer player could run faster than Ronaldo, jump higher than Ronaldo, or accelerate past Ronaldo. You could be forgiven for believing that he was built in a laboratory. Given his physical perfection, it's almost as if Ronaldo's been designed by a mad scientist intent on one thing: creating the perfect soccer player.

And what else would our mad scientist give Ronaldo? Talent. Plenty of it. Time and time again, this soccer GOAT has defied the laws of physics. From the streets of Madeira to the Santiago Bernabéu Stadium in Madrid, Ronaldo has wowed crowds with his powerful shots, dynamic dribbling, and close control. Ronaldo doesn't just have mad skills—he also has the ability to use those skills in the biggest moments for the biggest teams in the world.

Every individual must find their place in a team. And unlike *some* soccer players who have stayed at the same club for nearly all their career, Ronaldo has adapted his style based on the tactics of different managers in different countries.

He's faced opponents in Italy who love to defend, in England against defenders who push and shove, and in La Liga, where the defenders target key players. Ronaldo has succeeded everywhere he's gone. No matter what team he plays for, Ronaldo is the ultimate soccer GOAT.

But before you make up your mind, let me ask you this: If you were building the perfect soccer player in your laboratory, what skills would you give them that Ronaldo hasn't got? Exactly!

Seth
Machine v. human—no contest, is it?

Matt
Who said anything about Messi being human? The guy is a soccer GOD!

Seth
You sound like the only believer.

Matt
Well, you sound mistaken.

THE SCORES ARE IN:

	MESSI	RONALDO
PHYSICAL SKILLS RATING	8/10	10/10
TECHNICAL SKILLS RATING	10/10	9/10
TACTICAL SKILLS RATING	10/10	8/10
TOTAL SCORE	28/30	27/30

So, those are our ratings. But now the power is in your hands. Who do *you* think is the GOAT when it comes to skills?

My Skills GOAT is

....

HALFTIME

QUIZZES

Peep! We're going to need fifteen minutes to cool off. All that debating has got us worked up. Matt's heart is thumping and Seth is beginning to sweat. So while we head back into the locker room for our oranges and massages, we'll leave you with some halftime entertainment.

GENERAL KNOWLEDGE

1. Messi's favorite goal celebration—pointing to the sky with both hands—is a tribute to who?

....

2. Which poor Manchester United defender did young Ronaldo destroy during their now-famous friendly match against Sporting Lisbon in 2003?

....

3. How many Copa América finals did Messi lose with Argentina before he finally lifted the trophy in 2021?

....

4. Why did Ronaldo become England's public enemy number one in 2006?

....

5. During the time they both played in Spain's La Liga, one GOAT took more shots and the other scored more goals. Which is which?

....

MESSI OR RONALDO? OR BOTH?!

1. I have won the Champions League with more than one club.

☐ Messi ☐ Ronaldo ☐ Both

2. I have an Olympic gold medal.

☐ Messi ☐ Ronaldo ☐ Both

3. I am my country's top scorer ever at World Cup tournaments.

☐ Messi ☐ Ronaldo ☐ Both

4. I hold the record for scoring the most goals in men's international soccer history.

☐ Messi ☐ Ronaldo ☐ Both

5. I have played on the same team as Sergio Ramos, Ángel Di María, and Carlos Tevez.

☐ Messi ☐ Ronaldo ☐ Both

GENERAL KNOWLEDGE ANSWERS

1. His grandmother Celia • 2. John O'Shea • 3. Three • 4. He winked after helping to get his Manchester United teammate Wayne Rooney sent off in the World Cup quarter-final. • 5. Ronaldo took 618 more shots than Messi, but Messi scored 22 more goals.

MESSI OR RONALDO? OR BOTH? ANSWERS

1. Ronaldo • 2. Messi • 3. Messi • 4. Ronaldo • 5. Both

MESSI V. RONALDO

THE GREATEST-EVER CLASHES

It's a rare occasion that our GOATs face off against each other on the same field (usually no more than a few times a season), but that's what makes these occasions even more special.

So, what actually happens when Messi and Ronaldo go head-to-head on the soccer field? Well, we've selected some of their greatest-ever battles for your entertainment . . .

CLASH #1

A FIRST CLASH TO FORGET

BARCELONA 0 | 0 MANCHESTER UNITED

APRIL 23, 2008 • CHAMPIONS LEAGUE

OK, perhaps this isn't quite "greatest-ever" material, but it is a very important moment in our battle of the GOATs: their first-ever matchup! Ronaldo missed a penalty but made up for it in the second leg of this Champions League semifinal, with Manchester United going on to win 1–0. Unlucky, Messi!

CLASH #2

MESSI MOVES AHEAD!

BARCELONA 2 | 0 MANCHESTER UNITED

MAY 27, 2009 • CHAMPIONS LEAGUE

By 2009, Ronaldo and Messi were said to be the two best players in the world. This final was billed as a battle between the two—and Messi came out on top! He scored an incredible header to win the trophy for a dominant Barcelona side.

CLASH #3

MESSI THE PLAYMAKER!

BARCELONA 5 | 0 REAL MADRID

NOVEMBER 29, 2010 • LA LIGA

Our GOATs' first battle in La Liga definitely goes down in the history books. Both players had won the Ballon d'Or, and were desperate to prove themselves to be the best in the world. Imagine Ronaldo's surprise, then, as a ruthless Barcelona humiliated Real Madrid. Messi didn't score, but he did create two goals in a spectacular performance.

CLASH #4

RONALDO GETS REVENGE!

BARCELONA 1 | 3 REAL MADRID

FEBRUARY 26, 2013 • COPA DEL REY

After scoring a seventh-minute penalty, CR7 doubled Madrid's lead with a trademark header to eliminate Messi's team. Game on, Messi!

CLASH #5

MESSI CELEBRATES IN STYLE!

REAL MADRID 2 | 3 BARCELONA

APRIL 23, 2017 • LA LIGA

A five-goal thriller with a last-minute Messi winner? Delicious. And the celebration, where he held his shirt in front of Real Madrid's supporters? What more could you want?

CLASH #6

KING CRISTIANO!

BARCELONA 0 | 3 JUVENTUS

DECEMBER 8, 2020 • CHAMPIONS LEAGUE

Juventus needed a big victory to guarantee top spot in the group. There was just one problem: Barcelona had won twenty-five matches in a row in the Champions League group stage. Step forward, Ronaldo! After scoring an early penalty, Cristiano dispatched a second goal to send Juventus to the top of the group.

CLASH #7

NEW TEAMS, SAME GOATS

PSG 5 | 4 RIYADH ALL-STARS

JANUARY 20, 2023 • FRIENDLY

This was the first matchup of a new era for our GOATs. With Messi in Paris and Ronaldo in Saudi Arabia, there was a relaxed feel to this exhibition match. There was no shortage of entertainment, however, as Ronaldo scored two goals and Messi secured one.

So, that was a sweeping tour of Messi and Ronaldo's biggest and best battles, but who wins overall when our GOATs go head-to-head? Well, here's a handy table with the answer:

THE BATTLE OF THE GOATS: MESSI V. RONALDO

	MESSI	*RONALDO*
WINS	16	11
GOALS	22	21

Messi might be out in front when it comes to direct battles between their teams, but who will win the battle of the individuals? It's time to put your orange peel back in the box, have a last gulp of water, and then get ready for the second half. Let's goooo . . .

STATS

WHAT ARE SOCCER STATS?

Messi and Ronaldo are super-skillful players, but what makes them so special is their ability to turn that talent into soccer gold—game after game, season after season.

We know that Messi and Ronaldo have enjoyed incredible success over their careers, but which GOAT will come out on top in the battle of the statistics? We're talking goals, awards, and trophies galore! To make things "clear and obvious," as VAR (video assistant referee) would say, we're going to split the key stats into three main groups:

PERFORMANCE STATS
We'll look at the crazy numbers of goals and assists that make Messi and Ronaldo the best in the game.

INDIVIDUAL ACHIEVEMENTS
We'll add up the achievements—everything from the man of the match to the Ballon d'Or award.

TEAM STATS
We'll analyze the cups and league titles won, for club and country.

Remember: The stats don't lie . . .

PERFORMANCE STATS

MESSI

	GAMES	GOALS	ASSISTS
FOR CLUB	853	704	303
FOR COUNTRY	178	106	53
TOTAL	1031	810	356

RONALDO

	GAMES	GOALS	ASSISTS
FOR CLUB	949	701	201
FOR COUNTRY	203	127	34
TOTAL	1152	828	235

Let's start with the headline news:

- The GOAT with the most goals is RONALDO!
- The GOAT with the most assists is MESSI!
- The GOAT with the most goals and assists combined is MESSI!

Got it? Great! Now, let's dive deeper into the numbers.

CRISTIANO RONALDO

It's a ridiculously close contest, but Ronaldo takes the top prize for the total number of goals. No one has ever loved scoring quite as much as Cristiano does, in lots of different countries and in lots of different competitions. One competition stands out, however, as his clear favorite: the Champions League.

THE CHAMPIONS LEAGUE

	MESSI	RONALDO
GAMES PLAYED	163	183
GOALS	129	140
ASSISTS	40	41

Ronaldo is also the ultimate all-round scorer when our GOATs go head-to-head:

MESSI V. RONALDO

	MESSI	RONALDO
RIGHT FOOT	102	531
LEFT FOOT	679	154
HEADERS	26	141
TOTAL	807	826

Did you know Ronaldo has completed the perfect hat trick (one right-foot goal, one left-foot goal, one header) nine times in his career. And Messi? Never.

LIONEL MESSI

Ronaldo's stats might be good, but he has played more than one hundred more games than Messi has. And the bigger the game, the better Messi's stats seem to get:

THE WORLD CUP WIZARD

	MESSI	RONALDO
GAMES PLAYED	26	22
GOALS	13	8
ASSISTS	8	2

THE KING OF EL CLÁSICO

	MESSI	RONALDO
GAMES PLAYED	45	30
GOALS	26	18
ASSISTS	14	1

THE ULTIMATE BIG-GAME PLAYER

	MESSI	RONALDO
FINALS PLAYED	48	30
GOALS	35	22
ASSISTS	15	2

So, the question is: When and how did Messi become such a lethal goal-scorer? Well, it all began in 2008, when Pep Guardiola took over as Barcelona boss . . .

MESSI AND THE 91-GOAL MIRACLE YEAR

New Barcelona manager Pep Guardiola's first bold move was to get rid of the team's Brazilian superstar, Ronaldinho.

The fans were shocked—who was going to take his place and where were the goals going to come from now? The answer: Messi!

What, really? At the time, Messi was seen as a skilfull winger who scored goals, but not trophy-winning numbers of them. But Guardiola had big plans to turn Messi into Barcelona's main man.

In 2008, Pep handed Messi the shirt that had previously been worn by Ronaldinho. As part of the new role, Guardiola also gave Messi the freedom to attack in central areas, where there were better shooting positions. And the results were remarkable.

BARCELONA'S RESULTS, 2007–09

SEASON	*GOALS*	*ASSISTS*	*TROPHIES*
2007–08	16	16	0
2008–09	38	19	La Liga, Copa del Rey, and Champions League

The next season, Guardiola decided to move Messi from the wing to the middle of the Barcelona attack. And Messi's numbers got even better.

MESSI'S GOALS PER SEASON

SEASON	GOALS
2009–10	47
2010–11	53
2011–12	73

Whoa, seventy-three goals in a single season? Yes, and that was only for Barcelona—in total, during the year 2012, Messi scored ninety-one goals for club and country, a world record that will surely never be broken.

MESSI'S GOALS IN 2012

GAMES	69
GOALS	91
HAT TRICKS	9
GOALS PER GAME	1.32
SHOTS PER GOAL	3.81
MINUTES PER GOAL	65.3

NOW THAT'S WHAT WE CALL A SHARPSHOOTING STRIKER!

So, did all that extra scoring mean that Messi stopped setting up so many goals for his teammates? No, not at all. In fact, his number of assists increased too.

SEASON	ASSISTS
2009–10	12
2010–11	27
2011–12	32

WHO'S THE WINNER?

While Messi and Ronaldo like to score their goals in different ways, they're pretty much tied at the top when it comes to the numbers. Come on, 810 v. 828 goals is way too close to call!

When you throw in assists as well, Messi rises above Ronaldo, but let's look at some other ways of deciding who's the best.

INDIVIDUAL ACHIEVEMENTS

Who comes out on top in the battle for individual achievements? Here's a head-to-head look at how many awards our GOATs have won:

	AWARDS	MESSI	RONALDO
INDIVIDUAL	Ballon d'Or	8	5
	FIFA World Player of the Year	7	5
	FIFA Puskás Award (for world's most beautiful goal of the year)	0	1
CLUB	Champions League Final Man of the Match	1	1
	UEFA Men's Player of the Year	2	3
	League Best Player of the Year	6	5
	European Golden Shoe (for top scorer in Europe's top leagues)	6	4
	Champions League Top Scorer	6	7
	League Top Scorer	8	6
COUNTRY	World Cup Golden Ball (for best player)	2	0
	World Cup Golden Boot (for top scorer)	0	0
	Copa América/Euros Best Player	2	0
	Copa América/Euros Top Scorer	1	2
	TOTAL	49	39

Let's start with the headlines again:

- The GOAT with the most UEFA Men's Player of the Year awards is RONALDO!
- The GOAT with the most World Cup Golden Balls is MESSI!
- The GOAT with the most Ballons d'Or is MESSI!

LIONEL MESSI

Yes, Messi has won the Ballon d'Or eight times—that's three more than Ronaldo and five more than any other player *ever*!

WHAT THE DOUBTERS SAY

"It's a fix! FIFA makes sure that Messi always wins."

WRONG!

The Ballon d'Or award isn't chosen by the big bosses at FIFA; it's voted for by the best journalists from the world's one hundred top-ranked soccer nations. So there's no dodgy dealing here; Messi has just been the best player on the planet, year after year!

So, GOAT debate closed? Well, not if Ronaldo has anything to say about it . . .

CRISTIANO RONALDO

While he might not have won as many awards as Messi, Ronaldo has won a wide range of awards from all over the world. Plus, awards aren't the only kind of individual achievement in soccer; there are also records. And no one has broken as many records as Ronaldo:

- In 2012–13, he broke the La Liga record by scoring eight hat tricks for Real Madrid in one season!
- During the 2013–14 season, he scored seventeen goals in the Champions League, which is still a record.
- In 2015, he overtook Messi as the Champions League's all-time leading goal-scorer, and he still holds the record now, with an astonishing 140 goals!
- In 2018, he overtook Raúl to become Real Madrid's all-time leading goal-scorer, and he's still there at the top, with a phenomenal 450 goals!

And finally, the one we're going to focus on here:

- In 2021, Ronaldo fired his way past Ali Daei to become the leading goal-scorer in men's international soccer history . . .

RONALDO, THE RECORD BREAKER

For Portugal, the 2014 World Cup ended early, in bitter disappointment.

Despite Ronaldo's late winner against Ghana, his fiftieth international goal, Portugal finished below the USA and was knocked out in the group stage.

RONALDO FOR PORTUGAL, 2013–14

GAMES PLAYED	GOALS
114	50

Ronaldo went home feeling frustrated, but he didn't give up. No, he was determined to do better and to score *a lot* more goals.

BANG! He scored a hat trick against Armenia to help Portugal qualify for Euro 2016.

BANG! He scored two goals against Hungary to get them through the group stage.

BANG! He scored the crucial opening goal against Wales in the semifinals.

CHAMPIONS AT LAST!

Four days later, Portugal beat France in the final to become European Champions. Hurray, an international trophy at last!

And Ronaldo didn't stop there.

	GAMES	GOALS
2016	13	13
2017	11	11
2018	7	6
2019	10	14

Wow, that was fast—fifty-one goals in fifty-one games! By September 8, 2020, Ronaldo's Portugal stats had jumped once again.

CAPS	GOALS
165	105

Soon, Ronaldo was closing in on 109 goals, the men's international world record. By the end of the Euros, Ronaldo was tied with Daei at the top with 109 goals. But the question was, could he break the record in Portugal's next game against the Republic of Ireland in September 2021? Of course he could!

Ronaldo scored a header in the eighty-ninth minute—and he scored another just six minutes later. At last, he was number one—yet another world record was his. ■

WHO'S THE WINNER?

In terms of awards, Messi is the ultimate soccer GOAT, but no one breaks records like Ronaldo, and that's a key part of soccer history too.

So, the winner is . . . ? No, wait—come on, the vote for the GOAT has to be based on more than just individual achievements. Soccer is a *team* game, and no stat is more important than the number of trophies you win together!

TEAM STATS

		MESSI	RONALDO
CLUB	UEFA CHAMPIONS LEAGUE	4	5
	LEAGUE TITLES	12	7
	DOMESTIC CUPS	7	6
	FIFA CLUB WORLD CUP	3	4
COUNTRY	FIFA WORLD CUP	1	0
	COPA AMÉRICA/EUROS	1	1
	FINALISSIMA/UEFA NATIONS LEAGUE	1	1
	OLYMPICS	1	0
	TOTAL	30	24

So first, a look at the main headlines:

- The GOAT with the most league titles is MESSI!
- The GOAT with the most Champions League trophies is RONALDO!
- The GOAT with the most international trophies is MESSI!

Got it? Before we dive deeper into their personal achievements for club and country, however, we think we need to say a quick word about Messi and Ronaldo's incredible teammates.

As great as Messi and Ronaldo are as individual soccer players, you're going to need brilliant players alongside you on the field if you're going to win the top trophies.

PLAYED ALONGSIDE MESSI AT BARCELONA	PLAYED ALONGSIDE RONALDO AT REAL MADRID
Carles Puyol	Sergio Ramos
Jordi Alba	Gareth Bale
Xavi	Karim Benzema
Andrés Iniesta	Toni Kroos
Thierry Henry	Marcelo
Sergio Busquets	Xabi Alonso
Neymar Jr	Ángel Di María
Ronaldinho	Mesut Özil

What a list of legends—it's like a *Who's Who* of world soccer icons! Yes, teamwork makes the dream work, and to prove it, let's take a closer look at some of Messi's and Ronaldo's greatest team achievements.

MESSI AND THE BIG BARCELONA REBUILD

After the glory years under Guardiola (2008–12), the Spanish giants went through what they'd probably call a "bad patch."

Securing one major trophy and a league title in two seasons would be a dream for most teams, but this is Barcelona we're talking about! It was time for change, and time for a new all-star attack.

Messi would, of course, still be the main man, but he wouldn't be the only superstar forward anymore. Brazilian wonderkid Neymar Jr had already joined the club in 2013, and in 2014, Barcelona added the final member of their new front three: a young Uruguayan striker named Luis Suárez.

MIGHTY "MSN"

Messi, Suárez, Neymar—on paper, "MSN" sounded mouthwatering, but would the superstars all work well together on the field? The three South Americans formed a strong friendship right away, and once they'd found their best roles—Neymar on the left, Messi on the right, and Suárez in the center—they formed an unstoppable front three.

That season, they led Barcelona past Ronaldo's Real Madrid and all the way to win La Liga and the Copa del Rey—and to the Spanish Cup too!

In the final against Athletic Bilbao, Messi was Barcelona's man of the match with two great goals, including one of

the best solo runs you'll ever see. But Suárez and Neymar Jr played their part too, and they would soon get their chance to shine on the biggest stage . . .

One of the biggest tests for the MSN partnership came in the Champions League final against Juventus in 2014. Barcelona took the lead in the fourth minute

BARCELONA'S GOALS, 2013–14

	MESSI	SUÁREZ	NEYMAR
GAMES PLAYED	38	27	33
GOALS	43	16	22
ASSISTS	21	16	9

BARCELONA'S GOALS, 2014–15

	MESSI	*SUÁREZ*	*NEYMAR*
GAMES PLAYED	57	43	51
GOALS	58	25	39
ASSISTS	31	23	10

but—shock horror!—it wasn't a member of MSN who scored it. Instead, it was midfielder Ivan Rakitić, set up by Andrés Iniesta. What a talented team they were!

When Juventus equalized early in the second half, however, it was time for Barcelona's big-game superstars to step up and save the day. First, Messi dribbled forward and fired a shot at goal. Juventus's goalkeeper, Gianluigi Buffon, saved it, but Suárez was ready and waiting for the rebound. It was 2–1! Then, with seconds to go, Messi started a counterattack, which Neymar finished off. The final score was 3–1—what a nail-biter!

Hurray, Barcelona was the new Champions of Europe! After the match, MSN posed for happy photos together with the huge trophy. It was the perfect way to cap off their incredible treble-winning season.

So, what's the next challenge when you're Champions of Europe? Becoming Champions of the World, of course! Barcelona achieved that too, beating River Plate 3–0 in the 2015 World Club Cup final. And guess who scored all the goals?

- One for Messi
- Two for Suárez
- Plus two assists for Neymar

Three superstars working together to win all the top team trophies—now that's what we call a perfect soccer partnership! ■

RONALDO AND THE CHAMPIONS LEAGUE CHALLENGE

183 games played, 140 goals scored, five trophies lifted in just one tournament—they don't call Ronaldo "Mr. Champions League" for nothing. When it comes to Europe's top club competition, he's the king for sure.

Ronaldo first won the Champions League with Manchester United in 2008, but it was at Real Madrid that he really made the tournament his own. From 2011 to 2018, he scored ten goals or more in seven Champions League seasons in a row! But we've already talked about Ronaldo's individual stats; this section is all about what he managed to achieve with his team, so let's go back to the summer of 2013 . . .

Ronaldo has just finished his fourth season at Real Madrid with fifty-five goals in fifty-five games. But so far, despite his own scoring efforts, his trophy

count is just two—one La Liga title, one Copa del Rey, and zero Champions League trophies.

£84.6 million for that? No thanks! The Real Madrid fans expected more, especially during Europe's biggest club competition. Back in the 1950s, the club had won the Champions League five years in a row, then they did it again in 1966, 1998, 2000, and 2002. That makes nine trophies in total, but the fans had been waiting for their tenth, *La Décima* ("tenth" in Spanish), for over ten years. Come on, Real Madrid!

Ronaldo was desperate to win the Champions League during the 2013–14 season, and he wasn't the only one. His teammates all shared the same dream, and by putting the team first and working together, they were going to make it come true.

As soon as the tournament kicked off, Ronaldo got to work, scoring goal after goal: three against Galatasaray, two against Copenhagen, and two against Juventus. By the end of the group stage, he was on nine goals, and they just kept coming! He scored four against Schalke, one against Borussia Dortmund, and then two to beat Bayern Munich in the semifinals. Yes, Real was through to the Champions League final at last!

In the big game against their Madrid rivals Atlético, Real found themselves seconds away from defeat, but they refused to give up. Ramos scored an equalizer in the ninety-third minute, and after that, there was only one winner in extra time. Gareth Bale and Marcelo made it 3–1, then Ronaldo put the cherry on top from the penalty spot. They had done it: Real had won *La Décima* 4–1!

Phew! Job done, time to relax? No, as the team celebrated in the locker room, Ronaldo suddenly got serious. "How are we going to win this tournament again next year?" he asked. Ronaldo's teammates just laughed. ■

Unfortunately, Real Madrid didn't win the following year—Messi's Barcelona did instead—but in 2016, Real made it back to the Champions League final and beat Atlético again. And this time, they kept on winning.

BACK-TO-BACK CHAMPIONS

REAL MADRID 4 | 1 JUVENTUS

2017

This was Ronaldo's greatest performance on European soccer's greatest stage. As well as scoring two goals, he also received the Man of the Match award. But most importantly, Real Madrid became the first club to win back-to-back Champions League trophies.

THE THREE-PEAT

REAL MADRID 4 | 1 LIVERPOOL

2018

Bale was their two-goal hero this time, but the main thing was that the team had won three Champions League trophies in a row. The three-peat, tricampeón, the hat trick—call it what you will, it was a big deal, and Ronaldo was proud to have played a massive part in this piece of history with his team.

WHO'S THE WINNER?

Messi and Ronaldo have both achieved incredible things with their teams, winning enough trophies to fill entire museums, not just cabinets!

Yes, they've been fortunate to share the field with some very talented players, but they have earned their places as the superstars of these elite teams. Time and time again, in the biggest moments of the biggest games, Messi and Ronaldo have stepped up for their clubs and countries.

SO COME ON THEN . . . WHO IS THE STATS GOAT?

In this Stats section, we've looked at Ronaldo's and Messi's records for goals and assists, and what each player has achieved as both an individual and a team member. Now it's time to put all that learning into action and VOTE FOR THE GOAT!

Now over to Matt to make the case for Mr. Ballon d'Or himself . . .

MATT'S CASE FOR MESSI

- 810 goals
- 356 assists
- 91 goals in A SINGLE YEAR
- 12 league titles
- 8 Ballons d'Or
- 4 Champions League trophies
- And 1 WORLD CUP!

Messi's numbers speak for themselves, don't they? (No, apparently not. Seth says I'm just being lazy, so fiiiiine, I'll add some words to my argument.) Look, what more does a guy (or god, or alien—I'm still not quite sure) have to do and win to prove he's the soccer GOAT around here? Yes, Messi uses his left foot *a lot,* but if you had the greatest foot in soccer, wouldn't you use it as much as you possibly could? And yes, Messi spent seventeen years playing for Barcelona—one of the best clubs in the world—but he's so brilliant that he somehow managed to make them even better. And just look at what he did with Argentina!

Messi wins in almost every stats battle:

- More Ballons d'Or
- More team trophies
- More club goals
- More goals per game
- And way more assists

As top soccer writer Simon Kuper has said, Messi and Ronaldo "are the world's two best forwards, but Messi is also the world's best playmaker." A playmaker is someone who sets up goals for others—and Messi does this better than anyone else. That's why he's the soccer GOAT.

SETH'S CASE FOR RONALDO

Ronaldo's and Messi's goals per game are impressive, but they are far below those of Pelé, Eusébio, and Fernando Peyroteo (who scored a whopping 1.77 goals per game!). So the numbers alone aren't enough to tell the story (otherwise this would be a book about why Peyroteo is the GOAT). Instead, we need to go beyond the numbers to find the true facts.

What sets Ronaldo apart is his ability to perform on the greatest stage: the Champions League. In modern soccer, it is the Champions League that is the true marker of success. The best players play for the best clubs, and this makes the knockout rounds of the Champions League the toughest tests it's possible to have in soccer. And these are tests that Ronaldo has smashed time and time again.

Ronaldo was also the first player in history to win five Champions Leagues. He's also the Champions League's all-time leading scorer—with an incredible seventeen goals in one season! Yes, Messi's stats are incredible, but without teammates Xavi and Iniesta he's never made it past the quarterfinals of the Champions League. Ronaldo's talent has shone all over the world and he's won trophies wherever he's gone. He's also won the Champions League with *two* different clubs. Ronaldo is the GOAT when it comes to the stats that matter.

Seth
Messi has more Ballons d'Or? It turns out the stats do lie.

Matt
Hey, don't be a bad loser. Like Ronaldo.

Seth
I'm pretty sure it was Messi who quit his national team after losing a final?

Matt
Whatever, I've got two words for you: eight Ballons d'Or.

Seth
That's three words, actually . . .

THE SCORES ARE IN:

	MESSI	RONALDO
PERFORMANCE STATS RATING	10/10	9/10
INDIVIDUAL ACHIEVEMENTS RATING	10/10	9/10
TEAM STATS RATING	9/10	9/10
TOTAL SCORE	29/30	27/30

So, those are our opinions, whether you wanted to hear them or not. Now it's your turn to have your say! When it comes to the stats, who do *you* think is the soccer GOAT—Messi or Ronaldo?

My Stats GOAT is

. . . .

THE SOCCER GOAT
RONALDO
CONTRIBUTION
THE SOCCER GOAT
RONALDO

WHAT IS CONTRIBUTION?

Well, this is it, readers—our fourth and final section! Pages fly fast when you're having soccer fun, eh? In this section, we'll look at our GOATs' contributions to soccer—their overall impact, their legacy, and the many ways in which they've made the "beautiful game" . . . even more beautiful!

We all know that Messi and Ronaldo are phenomenal players, but how have they changed soccer forever? In order to answer that massive, scary monster of a question, we're going to break their contributions down into three key categories:

CLUB LEVEL
We'll look at the impact Messi and Ronaldo have had on the various teams they've played for.

COUNTRY
We'll review the impact they've had on their national teams.

THE GAME
And finally, we'll assess how they've changed soccer itself.

Got it? Good, let's gooooooo . . .

CLUB LEVEL

Barcelona, PSG, Manchester United, Real Madrid, Juventus—between them Messi and Ronaldo have played for some of the biggest clubs in the world and lifted all of the top trophies. Overall, our GOATs have made quite an impact at club level. Let's dive into the details.

LIONEL MESSI

When we think of Messi playing club soccer, we always picture him in a Barcelona shirt, don't we? In total, he spent twenty-one years in Spain—four in the club's academy, then seventeen in the first team. That's a long time for a soccer player to stay in one place! So what was Messi's impact on Barcelona during that time? Short answer: Totally revolutionary!

Long(er) answer: Before Messi joined the team, Barcelona was a talented but inconsistent group of individual players. With Messi, they became the best club team in the world. Messi's results with Barcelona are staggering. Let's take a closer look at some of their key achievements:

- Champions of Spain: ten times! (2004–05, 2005–06, 2008–09, 2009–10, 2010–11, 2012–13, 2014–15, 2015–16, 2017–18, 2018–19)
- Champions of Europe: four times! (2005–06, 2008–09, 2010–11, 2014–15)
- Champions of the World: three times! (2009, 2011, 2015)

With their world-class players and Pep Guardiola's revolutionary tactics, Barcelona became so successful that they influenced soccer teams around the world. Teams from Australia to Zimbabwe copied their pass-and-move tactics: playing out from the goalkeeper, dominating possession, tiring opponents out with lots of short passes, and then breaking lines with the help of a Messi-shaped magician. Soccer teams today still copy these tactics. Goodbye, hoofball. Hello, beautiful game!

Although Pep Guardiola's ideas were great, they mainly worked because they were built around one man: Messi. Even with all their incredible coaches and super-talented players, Barcelona relied on their number-one superstar more than anyone else. As players and coaches moved on to other teams and Barcelona started to lose a little (but not all) of their brilliance, Messi became even more important. So important, in fact, that there was even a word for it: *Messidependencia*—meaning "dependence on Messi."

If people make up words to describe how average your team looks without you, it's a pretty clear sign that you are quite important! With Messi, you can arguably go further than that and—to use another new word—call him a club-changer.

CRISTIANO RONALDO

Picture the scene: It's July 6, 2009, and Real Madrid's Santiago Bernabéu Stadium is packed with 80,000 people. But they aren't there to watch a game. Oh no, they've turned up to catch a first glimpse of their new world-record signing (for £84.6 million): Cristiano Ronaldo.

Under club president Florentino Pérez, Real Madrid signed the world's biggest soccer superstars. They'd been chasing Ronaldo for two years, and now they believed they finally had the missing piece in their quest for soccer world domination.

In a team of Galácticos (expensive, world-famous players), Ronaldo was going to be the biggest superstar of them all. And he had work to do. Real Madrid had suffered five consecutive Champions League defeats in the Round of Sixteen. The club was no longer dominant. Ronaldo, it was hoped, would change all that.

Some may have felt pressure. But not Cristiano. At his unveiling, Ronaldo smiled and waved at the delighted crowds. Weeks later, he made his Real Madrid debut in an impressive 3–2 victory over Deportivo La Coruña. And, of course, he scored.

WHAT THE DOUBTERS SAY

"Ronaldo has scored a lot of goals, but he's never transformed a team the way Messi has."

WRONG!

Ronaldo would go on to become Real Madrid's biggest superstar for nine seasons, scoring 451 goals in just 438 appearances. While the style and tactics of Ronaldo's Real Madrid may not have been as game-changing as Messi's Barcelona, their success certainly was. With two La Liga titles, three Club World Championships, and four Champions League trophies, Ronaldo more than paid back his transfer fee by returning glory to Real Madrid.

And it wasn't just the Real Madrid team that Ronaldo transformed in his career:

- At Sporting Lisbon, Ronaldo made headlines and opened the world's eyes to Portuguese talent.
- At Manchester United, he modernized the club, with coach Mike Phelan saying, "He took the players, the staff, the soccer club into a new dimension."
- At Juventus, Ronaldo transformed the club's off-field appeal, with shirt sponsorships almost tripling and online followers doubling.
- At Al-Nassr, he changed the face of Saudi Arabian soccer, with many other top players following him to the league.

Ronaldo also has an impressive record with his club teams:

- Manchester United, Champions of England: three times! (2006–07, 2007–08, 2008–09)
- Real Madrid, Champions of Spain: two times! (2011–12, 2016–17)
- Juventus, Champions of Italy: two times! (2018–19, 2019–20)
- Various, Champions of Europe: five times! (2007–08, 2013–14, 2015–16, 2016–17, 2017–18)
- Various, Champions of the World: four times! (2008, 2014, 2016, 2017)

If you want club success, who you gonna call? RO-NALDO!

WHO'S THE WINNER?

Sorry, this one's too close to call! Both GOATs have had an incredible impact on the club game, but in slightly different ways. While Ronaldo has transformed teams in multiple countries, Messi stuck with one club for twenty-one years. Which kind of contribution is better? It's very hard to say, so, for now, let's move on to the next category.

COUNTRY

At the international level, both players have enjoyed great success—Messi with Argentina and Ronaldo with Portugal. But what impact has each had on his country's soccer history?

LIONEL MESSI

For all of Messi's success with Barcelona, his journey with Argentina has been a lot more up and down. And until 2021, you'd probably say mostly down:

- Copa América finals lost: three (2007, 2015, 2016)
- World Cup finals lost: one (2014)
- Major international trophies won: zero

"Why doesn't Messi have the same impact for Argentina as he does for Barcelona?" the fans grumbled. "Is it because he doesn't care as much about his country?"

As we know, that wasn't true at all. And luckily Messi was finally able to prove it by leading Argentina—as captain and number-one superstar—to three major trophies in two years. With Messi,

Argentina won the Copa América in 2021, the CONMEBOL–UEFA Cup of Champions in 2022, and, best of all, the 2022 World Cup!

Yes, lifting the World Cup was one big team effort, but where would Argentina have been without Messi's seven game-winning goals and three astonishing assists? Nowhere near the final, that's for sure! To many fans, the 2022 World Cup felt like Messi's tournament, in the same way that the 1986 tournament in Mexico really felt like Maradona's.

While some Argentinians still prefer Diego Maradona for his incredible skills and passion, Leo has now made a similarly spectacular contribution to his country's soccer history. "Diego filled us with emotions. But between the cracks, without doubt, Messi is better than Maradona," said former Argentina player and Atlético Madrid manager Diego Simeone.

Messi has arguably brought more joy to soccer fans, but we'll leave the soccer-mad Argentinians to argue about that!

CRISTIANO RONALDO

These days, Portugal is a contender for every World Cup and European Championship, but in the past, they were never considered a giant of international soccer. For much of their history, they rarely troubled the top teams. In fact, before Cristiano came along, the top teams could have been forgiven for thinking that Portugal didn't even have a soccer team! Let's dive into the data.

PORTUGAL'S RECORD BEFORE RONALDO

WORLD CUP 1930	✗ Did not qualify
WORLD CUP 1934	✗ Did not qualify
WORLD CUP 1938	✗ Did not qualify
WORLD CUP 1950	✗ Did not qualify
WORLD CUP 1954	✗ Did not qualify
WORLD CUP 1958	✗ Did not qualify
EUROS 1960	✗ Did not qualify
WORLD CUP 1962	✗ Did not qualify
EUROS 1964	✗ Did not qualify
WORLD CUP 1966	Third place
EUROS 1968	✗ Did not qualify
WORLD CUP 1970	✗ Did not qualify

EUROS 1972	✕ Did not qualify
WORLD CUP 1974	✕ Did not qualify
EUROS 1976	✕ Did not qualify
WORLD CUP 1978	✕ Did not qualify
EUROS 1980	✕ Did not qualify
WORLD CUP 1982	✕ Did not qualify
EUROS 1984	Third place
WORLD CUP 1986	Group stage
EUROS 1988	✕ Did not qualify
WORLD CUP 1990	✕ Did not qualify
EUROS 1992	✕ Did not qualify
WORLD CUP 1994	✕ Did not qualify
EUROS 1996	Quarterfinals
WORLD CUP 1998	✕ Did not qualify
EUROS 2000	Third place
WORLD CUP 2002	Group stage

Portugal had only qualified for three World Cups out of seventeen! They also only qualified for three European tournaments out of eleven! Sure, Portugal is a relatively small nation of around 10 million people. And OK, compared to Brazil (215 million), Germany (83 million), and Argentina (46 million), it's harder to create a team of talented players. But something had to change. Step forward, Cristiano Ronaldo . . .

With Ronaldo in the red and green of Portugal, an amazing run of results began. Portugal not only qualified for every single international tournament they entered, but they also provided serious competition!

PORTUGAL'S RECORD WITH RONALDO

EUROS 2004	Runners-up
WORLD CUP 2006	Fourth place
EUROS 2008	Quarterfinals
WORLD CUP 2010	Round of Sixteen
EUROS 2012	Third place
WORLD CUP 2014	Group stage
EUROS 2016	Champions!
WORLD CUP 2018	Round of Sixteen
EUROS 2020	Round of Sixteen

Oh, and Portugal won the 2019 UEFA Nations League too! With more international appearances (205) and more goals (128) than any other player, Ronaldo truly was the difference. He had made it his personal goal for Portugal to become a force in international soccer.

"The achievement to win for Portugal is not the same for Argentina or Brazil or Germany," Ronaldo said. "It's more difficult."

WHO'S THE WINNER?

Arghh, it's another close call! (Yes, our behinds *are* getting sore from sitting on the fence!)

Both players have had massive impacts on their countries, bringing joy and trophies to the people back home. Ronaldo played a big part in transforming Portugal from chokers to European champions, while Messi finally lived up to being called "the next Maradona" by leading Argentina to World Cup glory. The winner? Wait, we've still got one more contribution category to go!

THE GAME

Soccer before Ronaldo and Messi was *very* different. These two haven't just taken the game to a new level—they've also pushed each other to ridiculous new heights. As future GOAT contender Kylian Mbappé has said: "I think Messi has done Ronaldo good and Ronaldo has done Messi good. For me they are the two best players in history . . . To have an equally good player in the rival team of the same league, I think the motivation is at a maximum."

The threat of Messi made Ronaldo work even harder in the gym and on the training field, while Ronaldo's achievements made Messi conjure even more magic with his left foot. And their ridiculous stats and legendary achievements aren't the only legacies they've left within soccer.

LIONEL MESSI

Soccer without Messi—it's hard to imagine, isn't it? No gliding dribbles, no impossible-looking passes, no whips of that beautiful left foot—what a nightmare world that would be! Even if you love Ronaldo, we can all agree that Messi makes soccer so much better, but in what ways has he changed the game forever?

STILL ROOM FOR THE LITTLE GUY!

There was a time in the late 1990s and early 2000s when it looked like small soccer players might die out like the dinosaurs. All over the field, in every position, players seemed to be getting taller and stronger every season. Was soccer just a game for the big guys now?

In 2004, along came a little Argentinian called Lionel Messi, just five foot seven inches tall (even after years of growth hormone treatment). He showed the world that size doesn't mean anything! If you anticipate what's about to happen so you're one step ahead, no one can stop you—not even the biggest, strongest center-back. And even if the big guys do get near you, they still have to get the ball off you! Messi's incredible skills are (almost) unmatched.

HOW ONE "FALSE NINE" CHANGED THE GAME

The role of the "false nine" has become a popular tactic in modern soccer—and that's mainly down to one player. It all began in 2009 during Barcelona's fierce showdown with Real Madrid . . .

MESSI: KING OF THE "FALSE NINE"

Collecting the ball deep in midfield, Messi had the time, space, and soccer genius to chip a perfect pass over the top of the defender so Thierry Henry could score. What an assist! Dropping deep again, Messi got the ball, played a lovely one-two with Xavi, and then slid a shot past Iker Casillas. GOAL!

Barcelona went on to win 6–2, but this game is not remembered for the scoreline—it's remembered because Messi discovered his perfect position.

Messi's new role was the "false nine"—a center-forward who is given the freedom to drop back into a deeper position on the field when needed.

After the game, the "false nine" suddenly became the most popular position in soccer, and it remains popular to this day. Although Messi makes the role look easy, it's actually really hard. Not many players are amazing creators *and* scorers—comfortable in the buildup and finishing chances in the box. But, after all, there's only one Messi. ■

CRISTIANO RONALDO

Those iconic stepovers, the tricks, the flicks, the piledrivers, and, of course, the iconic "*Siuuu*" celebration that follows . . . Even if you love Messi, we can all agree that Ronaldo makes soccer so much more exciting! But in what ways has he changed the game for good?

SOCCER, BUT FASTER, FITTER, STRONGER

Cristiano Ronaldo did not invent sports science, but he did take it to the next level. Ronaldo had seen the positive effect that living and eating smart could have on his performance, and so he knew it was in his power to reach new levels of soccer brilliance. This soccer GOAT is famous for the dedication he shows to the game:

- He plans the perfect gym program to strengthen his body.
- He takes his recovery so seriously that it's reported he has five naps a day!
- He uses a food scientist and employs his own personal chef to ensure his body is getting everything it needs.

As he evolved from a skinny teenager to a goal-scoring powerhouse, Ronaldo showed the world what's possible if you're willing to work for it. This was a soccer player who was faster, fitter, stronger, and more powerful than players of previous generations. If it worked for Ronaldo, it could surely work for others.

Because of Ronaldo's dedication to his body, other players have copied his training methods. Sports science has become so popular that it is now normal for soccer players to have their own chefs, personal trainers, and even sleep coaches. Due to Ronaldo's influence, athletes play at a higher intensity, moving the ball quickly around the field, and entertaining fans like never before!

REWRITING THE WINGER ROLE

In the early 2000s, soccer wingers had very specific roles. They were expected to beat the opposition's defenders and cross the ball for forwards to score the goals. But why was it only forwards who got to have all the fun? Ronaldo soon realized that he could score from the forward position *and* the wing. Over the course of his career, Ronaldo has transformed the role of the winger in world soccer. Take his first hat trick for Real Madrid, scored in 2010 against Mallorca . . .

THE RONALDO REVOLUTION

Sprinting forward from the halfway line, Ronaldo screamed for the ball.

Racing past the defenders, he received the ball on the edge of the penalty area and then coolly lobbed it over the keeper. GOAL!

When play resumed, Ronaldo started on the shoulder of the fullback (where you'd expect a winger to stand) and drifted centrally. Hang on—what was Ronaldo doing there?! Before the defense could react, Ronaldo chested the pass down and knocked the ball into the net. Another goal!

Standing on the wing, Ronaldo didn't seem too dangerous. Especially with three defenders around him! But this is *Ronaldo* we're talking about. He knocked the ball past the first defender, nutmegged the second, and then charged through the third. Faced with the keeper, Ronaldo carefully slotted the ball into the corner. GOAL!

Three incredible goals scored in three totally different styles! ■

Thanks to Ronaldo, modern wingers such as Mo Salah and Kylian Mbappé are now also goal-scorers. Rather than staying on the touchline, they run from wide into central areas, where they can score goals more easily. As a result, more teams play the formation 4-3-3, where the two wingers act more like inside forwards. All three attackers are capable of scoring goals, which means one thing for the defense: DANGER!

SO COME ON THEN . . . WHO IS THE CONTRIBUTION GOAT?

Well, before we make any final GOAT decisions, we'd like to talk about three ways in which Messi and Ronaldo have changed soccer *together*.

CONSISTENT SUPERSTARS, SEASON AFTER SEASON

In the past, most of the best soccer players would burn brightly for a few years, ten at most. But Messi and Ronaldo have been at the top for two decades.

Messi and Ronaldo were two of the first superstars to fully dedicate themselves to the game. They've both sacrificed *a lot*—fun nights out with their friends, big yummy dinners, sleeping in—to stay fully focused on being the best soccer players they can be. But hey, it was worth it, wasn't it? And thanks to them, most players now have the same professional approach to the game.

THE RISE OF BRANDS RONALDO AND MESSI

If Ronaldo and Messi do something, lots of other people also want to do it. These two superstars have the power to influence people all around the world—not just soccer players!

Ronaldo is the most followed person in the world on social media. Love him or hate him, people just can't get enough of him! And although Messi is a more private person, he also has hundreds of millions of followers. As a result, companies pay Messi and Ronaldo millions of dollars to promote products.

Our GOATs have seen how much money other companies make from using their names, so they have now started to make their own products. You can buy eyewear, underwear, footwear, blankets, hotel stays, perfumes, and even water with Ronaldo's CR7 branding stamped over it! Messi, meanwhile, has his own clothing line in the Messi Store. Our GOATs no longer just play soccer—they are superstars on the field and multimillion-dollar global brands off it!

PLAYER POWER

Years and years ago, people supported their local soccer team. Then, when television started to show matches, people could support any team. Now, thanks to Ronaldo and Messi, people don't just support teams—they support players!

From the deserts of Egypt to the rainforests of Brazil, fans wear the shirts of Ronaldo and Messi. Barcelona . . . Real Madrid . . . Juventus . . . Al-Nassr . . . Inter Miami . . . These days, soccer fans choose to support whichever team their favorite player plays for—and Ronaldo and Messi have more followers than any club in the world!

Increasingly, it is now the players who have the power, and that's all thanks to soccer superstars like Messi and Ronaldo.

In this Contribution section, we've looked at how Messi and Ronaldo have changed their clubs, their national teams, and the game of soccer itself. Now it's time to put all that learning into action and . . . VOTE FOR THE GOAT!

MATT'S CASE FOR MESSI

For me, there's no doubt about it: Messi has changed soccer more than any other superstar *ever*. Where would we be without him? Watching a very boring sport played by only big, strong guys, probably!

As Barcelona's superstar player, Messi successfully proved that skill and style were way more important than size, and that's only one part of his incredible impact on the game. There are also all the goals, the assists, the trophies, the magical moments, year after year, for both Barcelona and Argentina. One small man has made so much soccer history!

So what if most of his success came at just one club? Come on, why on earth would you leave Barcelona when you've helped turn them into one of the best teams of all time? And so what if he lost four finals with Argentina? It's not Messi's fault that his national teammates weren't on the same superstar wavelength! Plus, they won the World Cup in the end, didn't they? And the story is all the better for the setbacks along the way!

You might not believe in the perfect player, but I do. And his name? Well, let me give you a couple of clues:

- It isn't "Ronaldo."
- It rhymes with "dressy."
- Come on, can you guess what it is?

Not only is Messi the perfect "false nine," combining creativity with clinical finishing, but he's also the perfect professional, combining natural talent with hard work and dedication.

No player has ever shone quite as brilliantly and as consistently as Messi, and that's what makes him the ultimate soccer GOAT.

SETH'S CASE FOR RONALDO

Nobody has worked harder to change the game than Cristiano. Our Portuguese GOAT proved that there is no limit to your ability if you're willing to work for it. Other soccer players may have seen Cristiano's success and copied his training, but there will only ever be one CR7.

From his humble beginnings in Madeira, Ronaldo has conquered the world. In an era where the Champions League is the ultimate test of ability, he hasn't just succeeded, he's dominated! As the main man in a side of superstars at Real Madrid, he ended the debate of who the greatest-ever Champions League team is by winning it four times. He even won it at Manchester United!

People may ask where his World Cup is, but come on, Cristiano can't help where he was born. By winning the World Cup with Argentina, Messi has repeated history. Yet Cristiano has taken his nation to places they could never possibly have dreamed of. From rarely even qualifying for tournaments, Portugal has become a serious international force thanks to the brilliance of Cristiano Ronaldo.

Yes, Messi's contribution to the game is impressive. His contribution to *one* club is incredible. But Ronaldo's contribution to *multiple* clubs around the world is unrivaled.

Stick him in any team and Ronaldo will shine, whether that team counterattacks, dominates possession, or parks the bus. He'll probably break a record or two for them as well—after all, he is the ultimate soccer GOAT.

Matt
Tell me, what more could Messi possibly achieve in the world of soccer?

Seth
Messi hasn't even won the Euros—what a fraud!

Matt
Mate, do you even know where Argentina is?!

Seth
Does Messi even know what winning the Champions League five times looks like?

Matt
Good one—NOT! Thank goodness this is nearly over.

THE SCORES ARE IN:

	MESSI	RONALDO
CLUB CONTRIBUTION RATING	10/10	10/10
COUNTRY CONTRIBUTION RATING	9/10	9/10
GAME CONTRIBUTION RATING	10/10	10/10
TOTAL SCORE	29/30	29/30

So, those are our opinions, whether you wanted to hear them or not. Now it's your turn to have your say! When it comes to their Contribution, who do *you* think is the soccer GOAT—Messi or Ronaldo?

My Contribution GOAT is

....

EXTRA TIME
THE SOCCER GOAT
RONALDO

It's time for us to leave the field, and for *you*, the super-subs, to take over. So while we shake hands (unlikely), swap shirts (no chance), and head into

CHARACTER	Messi	Ronaldo
	He is shy, calm, and quiet, but highly competitive.	He is driven, determined, and confident.
	He has overcome setbacks time and time again.	He has overcome setbacks time and time again.
	He leads by example and inspires others to up their game.	He leads by example by setting high standards.

SKILLS	Messi	Ronaldo
	He might not be the tallest or the strongest, but Messi is usually the most agile player on the field.	He's so quick, strong, and powerful that his Real Madrid teammates nicknamed him "The Machine."
	He's an incredible dribbler, magical passer, and deadly finisher.	He's capable of scoring goals from anywhere with his powerful strikes.
	His brilliant soccer brain allows him to see things nobody else can.	He's adapted to teams in different countries and leagues, winning titles everywhere he goes.

the locker rooms, let's remind ourselves of the topics we've covered and the key points . . .

STATS

Messi	Ronaldo
He has a better goals-per-game ratio than Ronaldo.	He has scored more goals in total than Messi.
He has won eight Ballons d'Or.	He loves breaking records, including scoring the most goals in the history of the Champions League.
He has won more leagues and cups than Ronaldo—including the World Cup!	He was the first player to win the Champions League five times.

CONTRIBUTION

Messi	Ronaldo
He was so important to the Barcelona team that they created a word for it: *Messidependencia*.	He scored goals, won trophies, and broke records in five different countries.
He led Argentina to Copa América and World Cup glory.	He transformed the Portugal team into contenders for international competitions.
He proved that there's still room for the little guy in professional soccer.	He popularized the use of sports science in soccer, helping to create fitter, faster, and stronger players.

OUR RATINGS

	CATEGORY	MESSI	RONALDO
CHARACTER	PERSONALITY	9/10	9/10
	MINDSET	9/10	10/10
	LEADERSHIP	8/10	8/10
SKILLS	PHYSICAL SKILLS	8/10	10/10
	TECHNICAL SKILLS	10/10	9/10
	TACTICAL SKILLS	10/10	8/10
STATS	PERFORMANCE STATS	10/10	9/10
	INDIVIDUAL ACHIEVEMENTS	10/10	9/10
	TEAM TROPHIES	9/10	9/10
CONTRIBUTION	CLUB LEVEL	10/10	10/10
	COUNTRY	9/10	9/10
	THE GAME	10/10	10/10
	TOTAL RATING	112/120	110/120

Now, it's important to remember that those are only our opinions. The beauty of soccer is that *everyone* can have an opinion.

Seth
It's just a shame that some people's opinions are better than others'. Right, Matt?

Matt
Absolutely. Although it doesn't surprise me that someone who supports Peterborough United knows *nothing* about soccer.

Seth
Yeah, I forgot how desperate Messi and Ronaldo were to play for Southampton . . .

Before you buy the "Team Messi" or "Team Ronaldo" shirt, though, we've got two final pieces to help you make up your mind. From big breakthroughs to great goals and top trophies—there were just too many magical Messi and Ronaldo moments to include in one book!

So, before you make your final decision, we've selected a few key career highlights for you to enjoy.

MESSI'S TOP MOMENTS

KING OF *EL CLÁSICO*

REAL MADRID 2 | 6 BARCELONA

MAY 2, 2009

In his first game as a "false nine," Messi tore the Real Madrid team apart. He scored twice and Barcelona went on to win yet another Spanish league title!

ON FIRE IN THE CHAMPIONS LEAGUE FINAL

BARCELONA 3 | 1 MANCHESTER UNITED

MAY 28, 2011

Fierce rivals Barcelona and Manchester United met at the Champions League final to battle for the trophy. With the game tied at 1–1, Messi dribbled forward and fired a low, skidding shot into the bottom corner. Then, fifteen minutes later, Messi completed a magical run that set up David Villa to score Barcelona's third goal. Barcelona was victorious!

MESSI'S MIRACLE YEAR

2012—THE WHOLE YEAR!

With sixty-nine games played, ninety-one goals scored, and twenty-two assists, Messi was on fire during the year 2012! It's hard to pick just a few highlights but here goes:

- Fantastic free kicks against Real and Atlético Madrid
- A magical hat trick against Malaga
- Another hat trick, this time for Argentina against Brazil, including a stunning solo goal from the halfway line.

THE MAGIC OF "MSN"

BARCELONA 3 | 1 JUVENTUS

JUNE 6, 2015

Messi didn't score in his third Champions League final, but he was brilliant as part of Barcelona's new "MSN" strike force (Messi, Suárez, Neymar). With the match tied at 1–1, Messi set up the second goal for Luis Suárez, before Neymar added a third to secure the trophy.

A WORLD CUP (AT LAST)!

ARGENTINA 4 | 2 FRANCE

DECEMBER 18, 2022

After sixteen years of trying and failing, Messi finally won a major tournament for his country in 2021. Messi and Argentina soon won two more: the Finalissima (the match between the champions of Europe and South America), and then the biggest of them all, the World Cup! With the pressure on, Messi delivered his best performances in years and Argentina won on penalties. Hurray, Messi had the one major trophy he'd been missing!

RONALDO'S TOP MOMENTS

RONALDO THE RISING STAR

SPORTING LISBON 3 | 1 MANCHESTER UNITED

AUGUST 7, 2003

This was the night when Sir Alex Ferguson's mighty Manchester United got blown away by an eighteen-year-old wonderkid. Ronaldo played so well that Ferguson refused to leave Lisbon until a deal was done to sign him!

A MEMORABLE NIGHT IN MOSCOW

MANCHESTER UNITED 1 | 1 CHELSEA

MAY 21, 2008

Ronaldo's first Champions League final was a roller-coaster ride. After giving Manchester United the lead with one of his classic headers, he then missed from the spot in the penalty shoot-out. But luckily, so did John Terry and Nicolas Anelka for Chelsea! In the end, Manchester United was crowned as the Champions of Europe after winning on penalties.

PORTUGAL'S LEADER, ON AND OFF THE FIELD

PORTUGAL 1 | 0 FRANCE

JULY 10, 2016

Although Ronaldo was only on the field for twenty-five minutes of this Euro 2016 final, he still played a very important part in the game. When an early injury forced him off the field, Ronaldo became the team's coach and cheerleader instead. And it worked; Portugal scored the winner in the 109th minute, and Ronaldo hobbled happily around the field, celebrating a first international trophy!

MR. CHAMPIONS LEAGUE

JUVENTUS 1 | 4 REAL MADRID

JUNE 3, 2017

Of the six Champions League finals that Ronaldo has played in, this was definitely his star performance. He scored Real's first goal with an excellent low finish, and he scored their third too, after a bursting striker's run into the six-yard box.

RONALDO TO THE RESCUE!

PORTUGAL 3 | 3 SPAIN

JUNE 15, 2018

Who scored all three of Portugal's goals in this 2018 World Cup match? Yes, Cristiano! The first two goals were fairly simple, but the third goal was a Ronaldo big-game special. With his team losing in the eighty-eighth minute, he stepped up and curled a free kick into the top corner.

THE WORLD OF SOCCER DECIDES . . .

TEAM MESSI

"Messi is just special. I don't think we'll ever see a player like that again."

—DECLAN RICE

"I'm a big fan of Ronaldo, but I think Messi is the greatest ever."

—MARCUS RASHFORD

"Messi is alone in his class as a player. It is impossible that there is another like him."

—DAVID BECKHAM

"Messi is the best in history, no doubt."

—RONALDINHO

"I prefer Messi to Ronaldo, but Ronaldo is an animal."

—DIEGO MARADONA

"Messi is the best player soccer has ever produced."

—SERGIO RAMOS

"Of those I've seen play, Messi is the best in history."

—NEYMAR

"Everyone has an opinion but nobody can doubt Messi's there as the greatest of all time."

—PEP GUARDIOLA

As we mentioned earlier, we're not the only ones who can't agree on the question of the ultimate soccer GOAT! To help you make your final decision, we thought you might like a little help from some of the famous soccer players and managers who've been there and seen it all.

TEAM RONALDO

"Today, the best player in the world is Cristiano Ronaldo. I think he's the best because he's more consistent."

—PELÉ

"Cristiano is the best."

—ZINEDINE ZIDANE

"Training, professionalism, focus, motivation, success . . . Cristiano has an advantage over all the others."

—ROBERTO CARLOS

"If Messi is the best on the planet, Ronaldo is the best in the universe."

—JOSÉ MOURINHO

"Ronaldo was tough. He could play for Millwall, Queens Park Rangers, Doncaster Rovers, and score a hat trick in a game. I'm not sure Messi could do that."

—ALEX FERGUSON

"What Cristiano has done over the last 10–15 years, he's shown to everyone he's the best player ever."

—BERNARDO SILVA

"I think Ronaldo's output and actual numbers, and goals in big finals maybe give him the edge [over Messi]."

—FRANK LAMPARD

IN THEIR OWN WORDS . . .

"We fed off each other because we are very competitive. [Ronaldo] always wanted to beat everyone and win everything. It was a very nice period for us and for people who like soccer in general."

MESSI

"Whoever likes Cristiano Ronaldo doesn't have to hate Lionel Messi or vice versa, because they're both very good. They changed the history of soccer, and they keep doing it."

RONALDO

VOTE FOR THE GOAT

PEEP! That's it, folks; the final whistle has blown. We've done our best to set you up with everything you could possibly need to know about our GOATs and their . . .

- Characters
- Skills
- Stats
- Contributions

Now, you decide! Who's the soccer GOAT going to be—Messi or Ronaldo? Whether you choose to "*Siuuu*" for Ronaldo or point to the sky for Messi, it's important to remember that both these guys are *incredible*. Good luck!

My ultimate soccer GOAT is

. . . .